'Excellent, and very [...] in [...] craving 10p mix-ups, and fish and chips wrapped up in newspaper.'

JEN CAMPBELL, author of
Weird Things Customers Say in Bookshops

'Stack's brand of chummy 1970s and 80s nostalgia is amiable, and there is a lovely set-piece about dangerous childhood escapades on slam door trains.' *Guardian*

'For those of us still missing the Texan bar, Woolies and our C90 tapes, this charming, funny read will bring back some great memories.' BEN HATCH, author of *Are We Nearly There Yet?*

'When my copy arrived I thought I'd just flick through it but ended up reading it from cover to cover. Brilliant, funny and nostalgic. So much "I remember those!", shows I'm getting old. Highly recommended!' CLIVE BUCKLEY, Amazon reviewer

'Filled with all sorts of objects that I had completely forgotten about. Pure nostalgia for the 30-somethings.'

LILYLOULOU, play.com reviewer

'The kind of book that will inspire a warm glow of nostalgia.'
TIM ATKINSON, Bringing Up Charlie blog

'An excellent choice for your loved one's Christmas stocking, and certainly a damn sight better than that sodding meerkat book that a well-meaning associate of mine gave me last year.'

JONATHAN PINNOCK, author of *Mrs Darcy Versus the Aliens*

'I can't help it. I'm a child of the 80s. I love this stuff.'

[...]og

STEVE STACK

21st Century Dodos

A Collection of Endangered
Objects (and Other Stuff)

Illustrations by Dave Cornmell

The Friday Project
An imprint of HarperCollins*Publishers*
77–85 Fulham Palace Road
Hammersmith, London W6 8JB

www.thefridayproject.co.uk
www.harpercollins.co.uk

First published by The Friday Project in 2011

This edition published by The Friday Project 2014

1

A catalogue record for this book is available
from the British Library, whatever that means

ISBN 978-0-00-748466-9
Pi 3.1415926535897

Typeset in Minion by G&M Designs Limited,
Raunds, Northamptonshire
Printed and bound in Great Britain by
Clays Ltd, St Ives plc

MIX
Paper from
responsible sources

FSC
www.fsc.org

FSC® C007454

FSC™ is a non-profit international organisation established to promote
the responsible management of the world's forests. Products carrying the
FSC label are independently certified to assure consumers that they come
from forests that are managed to meet the social, economic and
ecological needs of present and future generations,
and other controlled sources.

Find out more about HarperCollins and the environment at
www.harpercollins.co.uk/green

By the same author

It Is Just You, Everything's Not Shit
Christmas Dodos

For Ethan and Martha
who have never heard of most of the things in this book,
the poor, deprived children

21st Century Dodos Online

I hope you like this new improved edition of 21st Century Dodos. If so, then feel free to interact in one or more of the following ways.

 www.facebook.com/21stcenturydodos

Come and say hello on the Facebook page where you will find articles, photos, links, discussions and competitions. Share your dodos with other readers and bother me with questions and comments.

 @dodoflip

Whenever I find anything dodo-related online, I will tweet a link. Feel free to follow.

 @dodoflip

If you have the Flipboard app for your iPad or iPhone then follow my feed for a fantastic interactive 21st Century Dodos magazine.

 Or you can email me at: 21stcenturydodos@gmail.com

Contents

Introduction   xiii

IN THE HOME   1
IN THE NEIGHBOURHOOD   15
ON THE HIGH STREET   49
AT SCHOOL   71
ON TELEVISION AND RADIO   87
AT THE CUTTING EDGE OF TECHNOLOGY   117
IN THE CINEMA   151
IN THE NEWSAGENT   167
ALL THE OTHER STUFF   197
READER'S DODOS   233

The End?   245
Further Reading   247
Thanks   249
About the Author   251

Introduction

For the paperback edition of this book (yes, there was a hardback – where were you?) I thought the least I could do was write a new introduction. Mind you, now I come to think of it, we are charging less for this edition so I am not sure I should be doing any extra work at all.

Oh well, I have started now so I might as well go on.

With *21st Century Dodos* I wanted to commemorate the many inanimate objects, experiences and, well, other things that many of us grew up with but which are either extinct or very much on the way out. Of course, most of these are victims of the eternal march of progress, and that is only to be expected, but it doesn't mean we shouldn't mark their passing and bid them a fond farewell.

I was heartened by the reaction to the first edition of the book. I was emailed, tweeted and Facebooked (that's not a word, is it?) by hundreds of people who wanted to share their thoughts and memories of some of the dodos included. I also received six photographs of white dog poo. Who said a writer's life wasn't glamorous?

But most enjoyable of all were the dozens of suggestions for dodos I had missed, and I am delighted to say that I have included as many of these as I could in the new Readers' Dodos section of this edition. Even more content for less money. I hope you are suitably grateful.

STEVE STACK
March 2014

IN THE HOME

Where we all grew up …

Rotary Dial Telephones

You know you are getting old when an everyday object you grew up with now looks like an ancient museum piece. Give a rotary dial phone to anyone under about 25 and they won't have a clue what to do with it.

Yet, despite the fact that phones haven't had dials for more than two decades, we still refer to dialling a phone number or dialling someone up. Curious, don't you think?

The physical act of putting your finger in a hole and moving the dial round meant that many frequently dialled numbers were fixed in our memories, far more so than in these days of speed dial and smartphones. And to prove it, you can probably remember the phone number of the house you grew up in, or perhaps your first boyfriend/girlfriend, purely because your brain has processed the movement so many times. How many numbers on your mobile contacts list do you know by heart today?

Still don't believe me? Try this: 01 811 8055. Ring any bells?

Rotary dials were essential in the early days of the telephone system as the exchanges operated a pulse dialling system. Each number was represented by a number of pulses, which is why when you dialled the number 5, you could hear five short clicks as the dial moved back round. But, as these networks were updated, we moved to tone dialling, which required buttons.

While this technological progress means we no longer get sore index fingers from repeatedly calling *Multi-Coloured Swap Shop* to speak to Bucks Fizz (see, you knew you recognised that number), and no longer suffer the physical agony of getting ten numbers into an international call only to misdial the last digit and having to start all over again, we now have to put up with the annoying 'Press 1 for customer services, press 2 for deliveries, press 3 to speak to an operator' and so on.

Not all progress is good.

Dodo Rating: 🦤🦤🦤🦤🦤

One Phone in the Home

Do these ring a bell? (Pun noted, but not intended.)

'Will you get off the phone? I'm expecting a call!'

Followed by:

'No, you hang up first … no, you … I'm not … love you … bye … bye … bye … are you still there? Yeah, me too …'

If they do, then you probably remember a time when most homes only had one phone. This was before the days of mobiles, of course. If you wanted to make a call you often had to do so in front of your entire family, something that could prove incredibly embarrassing to a teenager in the first flush of love or bloody annoying to anyone trying to watch television while mother hollered down the mouthpiece to a deaf grandparent.

Don't forget: no texts, no email, no instant messaging. If you wanted to speak to someone when you got home from school, or from work, then you had to do so using the only phone in the house.

That is, if your parents would let you, what with the cost of phone bills and all that. Nowadays kids spend more in a month on their mobile bill than our folks used to pay in a quarter for their landline.

Oh, how times have changed.

Dodo Rating: 🐦🐦🐦🐦

Trimphones

Nothing dates an object more quickly than futuristic design. Create a telephone in the 1960s that looks like it is from the 21st century, and by the time you reach the 21st century, it will look more like an object of the '60s than anything else from that time.

Such was the case with the Trimphone, an attempt by the GPO (before it was privatised and became BT) to create a luxury telephone for which they could charge more than the traditional rotary dial version.

The handset of the Trimphone (Tone Ring Illuminator Model) sat vertically on top of a body that resembled a slap of Cheddar cheese. The dial lit up when in use (although there was a health scare about the gas used to create this effect and it was removed from later models), and you could use the phone cradle as a handle to carry the whole thing about with as you chatted nonchalantly but in a futuristic fashion.

The Trimphone went through a few design changes from its arrival in the mid-'60s till they stopped making it in the early '80s, including a touchpad model and an array of designer colours. However, none of these could disguise the fact that a phone that looked cutting edge in 1965 had become something of an anachronism less than 20 years later. It was outlived by its rotary dial older brother.

Dodo Rating:

Directory Enquiries

Where we now have two very dodgy-looking blokes with moustaches in running gear harassing Ray Parker Jr and urging us all to call 118 118, we used to have delightfully well-spoken ladies at the end of the number 192.

'Hello, Directory Enquiries …' they would respond, albeit after what could frequently be a rather long wait for an answer, but the mists of nostalgia can allow us to conveniently forget such trifles.

The system was pretty much the same as it is now: you would give a name and possibly an address and the operator would try to track down the phone number for you. It used to be a free service, and was just one of many phone services that the GPO operated in the days before privatisation and deregulation.

There was the speaking clock, of course, which still exists. It started out in 1936 and the first voice was that of Ethel Cain, a telephonist who entered a competition and won ten guineas for her trouble. There have actually been only three other permanent voices for the speaking clock, which receives over 60 million calls a year, but there have been special one-off voices, including that of Tinkerbell during a Disney promotion.

But do you remember the old service that allowed you to call in and listen to the latest music releases? Or the one with football scores on a Saturday? There was even a Santa line at Christmas.

Many of these have fallen by the wayside now that we have clever phones and internet and, well, just don't use our landlines anywhere near as much, but the flurry of private directory enquiries numbers suggests that there is still plenty of demand for that service, at least.

Dodo Rating: 🐦🐦🐦🐦

Toothpaste Tubes Made of Metal

Kids today don't know how lucky they are. A simple push on a pump action dispenser and out spurts a minty worm of toothpaste.

Just give them a real old school tube of toothpaste, one made of metal, and let's see how they like that.

Toothpaste tubes first started appearing towards the end of the 19th century and prevailed right up until the Second World War, when metal shortages led to experiments with a plastic/metal mix. Metal tubes weren't finally phased out till the early 1990s.

Whatever the history, the point is that squeezing the last pea-sized bit of goo out of a metal toothpaste tube was one of the most difficult things an eight-year-old could ever be asked to do, especially if someone else has been squeezing from the middle. Woe betide the youngster who managed to split the tube while desperately squeezing, leading to tiny spurts of paste flying all over the place.

Gone, but not really missed all that much.

Dodo Rating:

Jif

Jif was the nation's favourite cleaning fluid, available in all sorts of sizes, shapes, and applications.

In 2001, the name was changed to fit in with Unilever's global branding for the product.

It is now called Cif.

Which is just plain silly.

(See also *Marathon* and *Opal Fruits*.)

Dodo Rating: 🐤🐤🐤🐤🐤

Creamola Foam

In an attempt to broaden the international appeal of this book, here is an entry for Scottish readers.

Creamola Foam was a powder that, when mixed with water, created a sweet fizzy drink. It came in lemon, raspberry, and orange flavours, with a cola version added later on. It was made by Rowntree's in Glasgow and, for some reason, and a bit like tablet and Edinburgh rock, never really made it down south.

Now, being from down south myself, I have never tasted the foamy delights of Creamola, so I asked my Scottish friend Kat to describe the taste for me:

> 'It's as if someone had made orangeade milkshake. Not very nice, now I think of it, but at the time, when I was seven, it was great.'

But in 1998, Nestlé (who had taken over Rowntree's) stopped making it.

In the more than a decade since, several petitions and online campaigns have been started to try to persuade the makers to bring it back. The issue was even raised in the Scottish parliament.

Now, I don't want to slight the nice people at Nestlé, whom I have taken the mickey out of elsewhere on these pages, but I would politely point out that no one wants a horde of angry Scotsmen chasing after them for any reason, least of all if they are demanding the reinstatement of their favourite effervescent fruit drink.

Fortunately, perhaps, for Nestlé, two Scottish companies have started making their own versions of the drink with both Kramola Fizz and Krakatoa available on shelves north of the border.

Still none down here, though.

Dodo Rating: 🐦🐦🐦

Milkshake Straws

You used to be able to get these from your milkman but I haven't seen one in years. Short paper straws, sealed at each end, they would contain flavoured powder – strawberry, raspberry, banana, all the usuals. The idea was that you tore off one end and poured the contents into a glass of milk, gave it a bit of a stir, and, voilà! – a tasty milkshake.

Of course, kids being kids, more than one straw in every batch would be unloaded straight into the mouth for a kick of pure whatever it was that went into these things.

Milkshake straws probably enjoyed their peak of popularity in the days of Humphrey, the mysterious milk snatcher in the Unigate TV ads (more on him later), his trademark red and white striped straw proving easy to promote to children.

Dodo Rating: 🐤🐤🐤🐤

Duo Cans

I'll be perfectly honest, I don't remember Duo Cans myself, but my dad suggested I put them in and, being the dutiful son, I thought it only fair and proper that I made the effort to research them.

And what a peculiar piece of ready-meal culinary genius they were too.

Basically a can of curry and rice that you opened from both ends – one end had the curry, the other had the rice. First, you had to heat it up by sticking the unopened can in boiling water. Once it was hot enough, you burnt off your fingerprints by opening this cylinder of molten metal – at both ends! – with a can opener then poured the contents onto your plate.

Hard to work out why they didn't last, really, isn't it?

Dodo Rating: 🐤🐤🐤🐤🐤

Black and White Television

You could be forgiven for thinking that black and white televisions were well and truly extinct, but you would be very wrong indeed.

OK, so there aren't *that* many of them around, but there are still over 25,000 people in the UK who own a black and white TV licence. It costs about a third of a colour licence, which may explain the attraction.

A fair proportion of black and white owners are elderly people who own an old set and haven't upgraded, but the old monochrome idiot's lantern remains popular with cheapskate students and for use on boats and caravans.

Colour television didn't really take hold in the UK until the late 1960s. Up till then, black and white held sway – it was the only option, and millions of homes had a set sitting in the corner of the living room. And despite the domination of colour in the 1970s, it was still fairly common to find black and white tellies in use, especially if you were visiting your grandparents, until a fair way into the 1980s.

Of course, by then it was a proper disadvantage to be devoid of colour, as this classic line from Ted Lowe during a snooker commentary proves:

> 'And for those of you watching in black and white, the blue ball is just behind the pink.'

The number of people owning a black and white licence is dropping by almost 10,000 every year, so we are very soon to see the eradication of this historic piece of technology. I trust we will all stage a minute's silence when that happens.

Dodo Rating: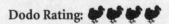

IN THE NEIGHBOURHOOD

*Where we walked and played, commuted
from, and came home to …*

IN THE NEIGHBOURHOOD

*Where we walked and played and commuted
from, and came home to...*

White Dog Poo

I am willing to bet that few entries in this book will get readers (of a certain age, at least) more nostalgic than this collection of paragraphs on dog shit.

The younger ones among you may find this hard to believe, but mention those three magic words to anyone over the age of 35 or so, and their eyes will glaze over, a strange smile will cross their lips, and they will be transported down memory lane to summer days of yesteryear when the nation's pavements were littered with canine fragrant parcels baking quietly in the hot sun.

You still see a lot of dog shit around these days, and frankly the culprits – or, more correctly, the culprits' owners – should be taken outside and shot, but the offending pile is usually a shade of brown. This was not always the case. There are no statistics available (which is a further outrage), but my completely unscientific method (which involves casting my mind back and having a guess) would suggest that around 30% of crap on the pavement pre-1985 was white.

Here's the science bit: dogs used to eat a lot more bone and bone-meal in days gone by. A dog with a bone is a classic image, but you don't actually see it in real life all that much any more. Bones, as any school kid knows, have lots of calcium in them, and white dog poo was basically the calcium left behind when all the other component parts of the turd had evaporated, been eaten by flies, or otherwise broken down.

We are also, as a nation, a lot more disciplined about picking up after our dogs, so steaming piles of doings are rarely left on the pavement for long enough to turn into ghost-like versions of themselves.

Fascinating, isn't it? Sort of.

Dodo Rating: 🐤🐤🐤🐤

Whistling

When is the last time you heard someone whistling? Think about it. I don't mean a quick wolf-whistle (although now I mention it, you don't hear many of them these days, either), or a builder sucking air through his teeth just before giving you an outrageous quote for a new extension, but a full-on, high decibel, cheerful tune from start to finish.

Chances are it's been a while.

But everyone used to be at it once upon a time: window cleaners, policemen, school janitors, milkmen, taxi drivers, all sorts of people. Now it appears to be something of a dying art.

Now, I accept that this won't be a source of regret to everyone. Miserable sods who don't like a cheerful tune emitting from 'twixt the lips of manual labourers are quite possibly overjoyed at the dearth of 'Waltzing Matilda's' or 'My Darling Clementine's', and that is fair enough.

Personally, as someone who can't whistle at all, I kind of miss it. Perhaps I could call upon the musically lipped readers of this book to pucker up and belt out a tune at some point in the near future, just to improve the rarity rating of this sadly neglected art form?

Of course, just because you don't hear window cleaners performing a wind solo while you walk down the street doesn't mean there aren't still people who take the fine art of whistling seriously. The International Whistlers' Convention takes place on a weekend in April every year, usually in Louisburg, North Carolina, although it tours occasionally and has been held in Japan and China – a truly global event. There are Child, Teen and Adult age groups, and entrants can perform in either Classical or Popular categories.

There is also a Whistlers' Hall of Fame which includes such luminaries as Bobbejaan Schoepen, Quingyao Cao, and Marge

Carlson. Their occupations are not given but I am guessing at least one of them is a milkman.

Dodo Rating: 🐥🐥🐥

Bob-a-Job Week

From the end of the Second World War right up to the mid-1990s, Bob-a-Job Week thrived around the country. Cubs and Scouts would roam the neighbourhood, knocking on doors and offering to do any odd jobs in return for a nominal payment – the 'bob' in Bob-a-Job being slang for an old shilling.

Washing cars, mowing the lawn, walking the dog, helping the elderly with their shopping, anything was up for grabs. One Scout troop even cleaned jumbo jets at Heathrow, although they probably got paid a fair bit more than five pence for that. Unless they were cleaning Ryanair planes, in which case Michael O'Leary would almost certainly have charged them for the privilege.

It was a great concept and very much a win-win situation. The Scouts raised some money for new woggles or books about knots, and members of the public got some annoying jobs sorted out for a pittance.

Sadly, the practice died out as our country became more and more obsessed with child safety, and the idea of unaccompanied children knocking on the doors of strangers didn't seem such a good one any more.

It is, however, scheduled to return, albeit in a new form. The Scout Community Challenge will involve groups of Cubs and Scouts, rather than individuals or pairs, teaming up to work on community projects. Quite how that helps the old dear who has been waiting for nearly 20 years for a nice young man to clean her windows remains to be seen.

Dodo Rating: 🐦🐦🐦🐦

Raleigh Chopper

The Chopper was, without any shadow of a doubt, *the* bike of the 1970s.

Designed to echo the look and feel of a chopper motorcycle (think *Easy Rider*), it was the coolest bike on the streets. It was also the most impractical.

The laid-back aesthetics led to an unstable ride, especially at speed. The high-backed saddle was great for giving 'backsies' but that made it even more accident-prone and, if you ever dismounted at speed, the gear stick was strategically placed to castrate the male rider. The rear wheel was larger than the front and the high handle-bars made few riding positions comfortable for more than a few minutes.

All that aside, it became a cultural icon and was the ubiquitous mode of transport for the suburban '70s teenager.

By the time the 1980s came round, the Chopper was overtaken by BMX culture. The appetite for bunny hops, 360s, and half pipes rendered the Chopper obsolete. That, and the desire to cycle for more than half a mile without killing yourself.

Believe it or not, the Chopper was relaunched in 2004 with a tweaked (for which, read 'boring') design. The seat had been lowered to discourage passengers and the gear controls were moved to the handlebars. Sensible, but dull. It has not made a significant impact.

Dodo Rating: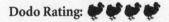

Raleigh Grifter

For a bicycle that was only manufactured for seven years (1976–1983) the Raleigh Grifter has left a remarkable impression and is fondly remembered by people (OK, mostly men) of a certain age.

Pitched as the younger brother to the Chopper, it was a far more practical bike, even if it was very chunky and heavy. The stand-out feature was that the gears, all three of the blighters, were controlled from the handlebar grip, as close to a motorbike throttle as a 12-year-old was likely to get in the days before joyriding and petty vehicle theft.

Looking back, the Grifter was really a simplistic hybrid of a BMX and a mountain bike, and may have played a small part in the success of the latter in the years that followed. After riding a Grifter, the move up to a racer was not quite as satisfying.

Dodo Rating:

Roller Skates

Everyone had roller skates when I was growing up. Learning to skate was a rite of passage similar to learning to ride a bike. Kids would start early with a pair of Fisher Price plastic jobs that could be adjusted as your feet grew. You then graduated to a rickety metal pair that, likewise, could increase in size as you went up the scale of that foot measurement thing in your local shoe shop.

Such childish toys were mere piffle, however, when compared to your first pair of roller boots. Fashionable (then, at any rate), sporty boots with integrated rubber wheels and a front stopper were *the* skates to have.

Any summer weekend in the suburbs you would see kids star-fishing their way down the pavement as they desperately tried to stay upright, two purple patches on their knees where grazes had scabbed over.

But more serious skaters wouldn't be seen dead on an actual pavement; oh no, they could instead be found spinning, pirouetting, and gliding backwards effortlessly in the local park, along the seaside esplanade (the wearing of a Walkman playing disco music was compulsory), or, of an evening, at the roller disco, many of which had sprung up in out-of-town shopping centres.

Then, along came rollerblades, the grey squirrel to the roller skates' red, and almost overnight it became dreadfully uncool to be seen with four wheels, one at each corner of your foot. A strip of wheels down the middle of a sturdy plastic boot was the only acceptable formation.

The roller skate was consigned to the dustbin of time, making only occasional appearances since. Even Andrew Lloyd Webber's dreadful musical *Starlight Express*, originally conceived as a roller skate theatrical extravaganza, converted to rollerblades, and that, as they say, was that.

Dodo Rating: 🐤🐤🐤🐤

Ring Pulls

For decades, the holy trinity of pavement litter was cigarette butts, blackened wads of chewing gum, and drink can ring pulls. Since 1989, these have been reduced to a double act only.

Younger readers, by which I mean anyone under the age of about 30 (most of whom won't be reading this book anyway), may be unaware that the ring pulls on beverage cans – Coke, Fanta, whatever – used to come right off the can.

That's right, clean off.

They were usually thrown away, often in complete disregard of the little stick man next to a wire bin who wanted us to Keep Britain Tidy, and were a common sight on pavements and kerbsides everywhere.

This removable ring pull, or pull tab, was invented in 1963 by a man with the wonderful name of Ermal Cleon Fraze. Prior to that time, cans had a variety of opening mechanisms; the most common of which was just to punch two holes in the top. Ermal's idea quickly caught on and became the standard for many years.

It was not without its problems, however. The edge of the tab, the bit that looked like a tongue, could be quite sharp and often resulted in cut fingers. This was before the days when everybody sued everybody else for the slightest injury, no matter how bloody stupid the injured party may have been, so that alone did not warrant sufficient reason for change.

Having been removed, it wasn't that difficult to pop the ring pull back into the can. Which was a good way to avoid littering the streets but not so great if you forgot it was there and swallowed the blighter.

And then there was that litter issue. Millions upon millions of ring pulls covered our streets. You couldn't walk down any suburban road without spotting them. They were the postman's red elastic bands of their day.

So in many respects, it was a good thing that the stay-on-tab was invented. Actually, the technology existed as early as 1975 (it was designed by a chap with another splendid name, Daniel F. Cudzik) but it wasn't adopted as standard in the UK until 1989. By the time the '90s hit, the road sweepers of Britain had disposed of nearly all the remains, any new sighting causing great excitement, as if it were a historic fossil find.

But progress does have a way of running roughshod over traditions of cultural importance, and the death of the ring pull is not without its cost.

We have lost, for example, the ability to disconnect the ring from the tab, slot one into a notch in the other and create a flying saucer/discus/ninja throwing star that zooms across the room. It was a special skill that took, ooh, minutes to learn but years to perfect. I will never be able to pass on this considerable talent to my own children.

And then there is the small matter of love. Yes, love, I tell you.

Numerous pretend playground weddings took place between junior school boys and girls, and were marked by the placing of a ring pull on the finger. It was a moment of romantic innocence and we shall not see the likes of it again.

I think you'll find that it is a statistical fact that divorce rates have gone up since the ring pull became extinct.

Coincidence? I think not.

Dodo Rating:

Cap Guns

Before it became frowned upon for small children to walk around pretending to shoot each other with realistic guns that created loud explosions, cap guns were as common as, well, bows and arrows with suction cups on the end.

For those unfamiliar with the concept (the girls, mainly – sorry, but it's true), these were toy guns made to look like classic Western revolvers (and sometimes other models) into which you loaded a strip or ring of caps which, when struck by the gun hammer, made a satisfying snappy bang and emitted a puff of smoke, similar to the bang of a Christmas cracker, but with more menace.

Ring caps were little plastic capsules containing a tiny amount of explosive (so small as to be completely safe) that were pressed into the revolver cylinder and set off one by one when you pressed the trigger. The process of loading them was more like loading a real gun but they only gave you six shots.

More progressive junior gunslingers used strip caps, a thin paper ribbon punctuated every third of an inch or so with a full stop of explosive. When the hammer hit one of these, the strip advanced along one step ready for the next shot. A strip could hold hundreds of caps, which allowed for lots of rapid-fire action, but did mean your gun always looked a bit odd with what appeared to be a paper streamer flying around behind it.

Personally, I preferred the strip caps, but only because you could unravel them, spread them across the floor and run a stone along them to let off a whole volley of bangs in one go.

Whatever your chosen ammunition, it didn't really matter. Whoever you shot would claim that you missed them anyway.

Tragically, the kids of today have graduated to real guns, and with those you cannot pretend the bullet missed you.

Dodo Rating: 🐦🐦🐦🐦

Routemaster Buses

Although ostensibly a London bus, the Routemaster with its driver/conductor team, hand-rolled route number indicator, and hop-on-hop-off doorway, has become an icon, instantly recognisable across the globe. It is the bus that all toy buses are based on, the bus that children draw with crayons, the bus that is emblazoned across souvenirs and which appears in countless film scenes where the director requires a shot that instantly says 'London'.

Remarkably, despite the fact that Routemasters regularly drove up and down London streets until the end of 2005, the last one was manufactured as long ago as 1968. Launched in the late '50s, they were made for just over ten years; 2,876 rolling off the production line in that time. It is a testament to their robust design and popularity that they hung around for so long.

Originally, the Routemaster was intended as a replacement for an ageing and expensive fleet of trolley buses and trams. It could hold 64 passengers, which was more than its predecessor, and weighed less, so was much cheaper to run. It was also remarkably light on its feet, making it an easier vehicle to drive. The driver was cut off from the passengers in his own cab at the front, and a separate conductor at the back sold tickets, helped old ladies with their shopping, and gave young scallywags a clip round the ear.

The most notable feature of the Routemaster was the open platform which allowed passengers to jump on and off, even if the bus wasn't at a designated stop. This was back in the days when running for a bus was actually quite a good idea because, providing the traffic was slow and you had a reasonable turn of foot, you actually stood a chance of catching up with it and jumping on.

Of course, the open platform also meant it was a lot easier to fall off, and most Londoners have stories of poor unfortunate travellers who came a cropper. And then there were the cheeky oiks who would jump on for a free ride until the conductor noticed them and shooed them off.

London Transport started to introduce one-person operated buses in the 1970s, with many single-deckers being put into operation, but the Routemaster still hung on to many routes, especially in the centre of London. Even privatisation in 1984 didn't kill them off, with many of the new companies refurbishing these buses from the '60s and giving them a fresh lease of life.

In fact, these legendary vehicles survived well into the 21st century, when the then mayor of London, Ken Livingstone, ordered their decommissioning. This coming from a man who, just a few years before, had said that 'only some sort of ghastly dehumanised moron would want to get rid of Routemasters'. To be fair, the main reason for the move was the need for disabled access to buses – the one thing the Routemaster could not offer.

The last route to be served by a Routemaster was the 159 from Marble Arch to Streatham, and the final journey took place on 9 December 2005. Such was the public interest that crowds flocked the route and sometimes even blocked the road. Hundreds of people turned up to bid a much-loved bus a fond farewell.

The Routemaster has not completely vanished. In London they are used for two special heritage routes, the 9 from Olympia to Aldwych and the 15 from Trafalgar Square to Tower Hill. There are also examples of the vehicle elsewhere in the country, with many local firms buying up stock as it was decommissioned. So there is still a chance to see a few of them for a while yet.

And in 2012, the new London mayor, Boris Johnson introduced an updated version of the Routemaster. The sleek new design is very modern, but keeps the classic open platform – something old, something new.

Dodo Rating: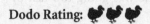

Bus Conductors

'Fares, please!'

When is the last time you heard that cry? I suspect you'll be hard pushed to remember. I am willing to bet it was some considerable time ago.

Next time you find yourself singing 'The Wheels on the Bus' to a child, and at some point in your life that is pretty much bound to happen, stop when you get to this line:

'The conductor on the bus says, "move along please".'

And ask the child what a bus conductor is. They won't know!

We are all aware why there are no longer any bus conductors; since the privatisation of public transport, companies have tried to save money and operating a bus with one person costs less than employing two, but the slow extinction of the role has sort of gone unnoticed.

The bus conductor's main job was, obviously, to sell and check tickets, but the role was much bigger than that. Think about that name, conductor, like in an orchestra. He or she would organise their passengers into some kind of order. They would make sure everyone who needed a seat could get one, that nursery rhyme cry of 'move along please' would ensure new passengers could get on, they would make certain that smoking only took place on the top deck, that unruly schoolkids got a clip round the ear to keep them in check, that fare dodgers were kicked off, that everyone knew what stop was coming up, and, something people tend to forget, they would keep the driver in check, quite happy to have words if he was going too fast or turning corners too sharply.

The bus conductors did their best to instil order and safety. They were, much of the time, a reassuring presence. Now you think about it, you probably realise that you miss them.

Dodo Rating: 🐥🐥🐥🐥

Playing in the Streets

In his excellent book, *How to Live Dangerously*, author and social commentator Warwick Cairns points out that our modern-day fears for child safety are largely nonsense. He calculated that if you actually wanted your child to be abducted, then you'd have to lock them out of the house for close to 200,000 years before they would (statistically) be taken.

And even then, the chances are they'd be returned within 24 hours.

Now, I don't want to belittle the many horrible things that happen to children, but the facts are that the vast majority of them happen inside the home, and are caused by members of the family. Playing outside, I would argue, is no less safe than it ever was. And yet children growing up today have less freedom to do so than ever before.

I grew up in the 1970s. I was allowed to play outside my house, a quiet but not secluded suburban street, from an early age. I was walking to school on my own by the time I was about seven or eight. And this was not in any way remarkable at the time. At ten I would spend most of the weekend out of the house, visiting friends, down the park, or climbing trees. As long as I was home for lunch and dinner, no one seemed to mind. Blimey, when I was eleven, I had a two-hour journey to school that involved a bus and a train – and that train was one of the old ones where you could open the doors at any time, and with carriages full of schoolkids, they were pretty much open for most of the journey.

Nowadays, allowing your seven-year-old to walk to school alone can result in disapproving comments from other parents, a local newspaper headline, and a radio phone-in.

I remember some years ago allowing my young son to go unaccompanied to the toilet in a restaurant. The people we were with were astounded that I could be so reckless: they were assuming that some nutter was lying in wait to abduct him in a branch of Pizza Express.

What has become of us?

The world is no more dangerous now than it was when I was young; if anything, it is safer. Cars are safer, roads are safer, neighbourhoods are safer – and yet kids under the age of eight are rarely allowed outside unaccompanied. Forgive the rant, but I fear for the sort of mollycoddled children we are raising today. Danger and risk are a part of life. Exposure to them helps us to judge and react to them. It builds our common sense. They are, I would argue, essential to growing up.

We should allow our children to play in the streets, climb trees, walk to school, play down the park, cycle round the neighbourhood, go to the corner shop, etc. They will become better adults as a result.

I was chatting about this very subject with an elderly lady a while ago. She told me how, in the late 1940s, she and her sister, both under 14 at the time, had travelled to Norway alone to visit family friends. Their parents waved them off at the garden gate and didn't see them again for nearly a month. They negotiated a train and ferry to Norway and then the journey through a foreign country to their destination and no one batted an eyelid. If that happened today, the parents would be arrested.

Dodo Rating: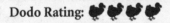

Election Vans with Loudspeakers

Before the days of 24-hour news channels, Twitter, and all things internet-related, politicians had to really put in some graft if they wanted to be elected. There was the door-to-door canvassing, the kissing of babies, and driving around in a van that had a loud-speaker on the roof.

It sounds daft now, if you have never seen such a thing, but it was standard procedure at the time. Seriously.

A big speaker or loudhailer would be strapped to the roof of an available vehicle, and the prospective MP would be driven around town while trying to convince people to vote for him or her. Usually this involved inspired and unforgettable rhetoric, such as, 'Vote for Peter Jones, I'm the man for you' or some such nonsense.

It was like the ice cream van of your nightmares.

Usually the arrival of said van would be greeted by jeers from builders hanging off scaffolding (if it was a Tory candidate) or a disapproving look from posh women in headscarves (if Labour). I presume it must have had some effect, though, as politicians did it for years.

Now they just poke you on Facebook or something.

Dodo Rating:

34

Nuns

There simply aren't as many nuns as there used to be, and their numbers are declining at an alarming rate. During the time John Paul II was Pope, the total of Catholic nuns dropped by a quarter. Between 2005 and 2006 (the most recent statistics available) the number of men and women belonging to religious orders declined by 10% – that was in one single year!

The reasons for this are obvious and twofold. First, and this isn't meant to sound flippant, lots of them are dying as they are an ageing population. Second, fewer women are choosing to dedicate their life to their God in this way. This combination means that nuns really are an endangered species.

Prior to the 21st century, most towns of a reasonable size would have some nuns knocking around. They were a bit of a novelty, I grant you, but not an uncommon sight. The arrival of a group of nuns in a public place would have an amusing effect on those around. Schoolboys and girls would often have a fit of giggles, women would look on curiously, and even the roughest bloke would turn into a true gentleman, 'Let me get the door for you sister' and that sort of thing. They would, usually, brighten up the immediate vicinity and leave politeness in their wake.

Now you are more likely to spot one on a *Nuns Having Fun* calendar than in the butcher's buying a pound of sausages.

Dodo Rating: 🐓🐓🐓

Telephone Boxes

When you think about it, it is a bit odd to get all misty-eyed about objects that were more often than not vandalised, frequently littered with prostitute calling cards, and usually smelt of piss. But there is no accounting for nostalgia, it is a powerful beast.

There are, of course, still telephone boxes around, but nowhere near as many as there used to be. And for good reason – no one uses them any more.

A recent survey revealed that only 3% of British adults had used a payphone in the past month. Statistics from Wales (hey, I take whatever I can get when it comes to stats) show that a quarter of phone boxes in the country made, on average, fewer than one call a month.

The reason for this is both obvious and understandable: 90% of adults own mobile phones. Mobile tariffs have become cheaper, with most people paying a certain amount a month to cover a bundle of calls and texts, and there just isn't the need to nip to a phone box any more.

So who is using them?

Well, the 10% of adults who do not own a mobile are certainly high on the list. As are foreign workers calling home. International calls on mobiles are still prohibitively expensive, so many of the migrant workers living in the UK find it cheaper to call from a phone box.

There is also the element of privacy. If you are lucky enough to find a classic red phone box, then you will be locked within a soundproof booth of cast iron, and passers-by will struggle to hear a word you say. For this reason they remain popular with individuals of a less savoury nature who 'need to speak to a man about a dog', or something like that.

But phone box use is plummeting, and long gone are the days when, and some of you will remember that this did actually happen, there would be a queue outside the local public telephone, with some old bloke getting impatient with the teenager calling his girlfriend from inside and taking ages to say goodbye. Older readers will also remember the days when the phones accepted 2p, a couple of which would more than cover the cost of your call. Minimum charge is 60p nowadays. Last time I used one, it was 20p.

When most of us think of a telephone box, an image of the classic red kiosk will come to mind. The first of these was designed in 1924 by Sir Giles Gilbert Scott, in response to a competition. The City of London was not keen on the concrete booths that had starting popping up around the country, and wanted something more stylish and, well, London-y. Scott's design beat two others and became known as K2 (Kiosk 2), quickly replacing the K1, although the box that appeared on the streets was not quite as the designer expected. He had specified a steel construction with silver paint and a blue/green interior, the final kiosk was, as we know now, made of cast iron and painted a bright red.

There were many incarnations of this original design, with the K6 being the one that was used most widely outside of London, and being the version that most readers will remember calling their boyfriends or girlfriends from, or phoning a cab from while pissed, or having a sneaky wee in … while pissed.

Since the late '80s, and the privatisation of telecommunications, the red phone boxes have been superseded by the rather dull metal and glass structures and also open booths. For a while, companies other than BT started putting boxes up, but they didn't last long. Now even these more modern versions are on the downturn; between 2005 and 2008 total phone box usage halved. It is probably fair to speculate that it has at least halved again since then.

As it costs £700 a year to maintain a single telephone kiosk, it is understandable that their numbers are dwindling, and it is to the credit of BT that they haven't scrapped them completely, recognising that they have to cater to the minority of people who still use them and acknowledging their social importance.

But that hasn't stopped them from decommissioning loads of old boxes and flogging many of them off for private use. Local communities have taken over the running of some kiosks and there are old red phone boxes in use today as libraries, grocery shops, tourist information booths and, in one case, to store a defibrillator.

With two-thirds of all telephone boxes making a loss, it is inevitable that their number will decline further, but over 2,000 have been given listed status so we should still see them around for some time to come.

Dodo Rating: 🐦🐦

Rag and Bone Men

You could consider them the first generation of recyclers. Men with a horse and cart would drive around the neighbourhood at slow speed, shouting, 'Rag and bone!' or some such cry, in an attempt to lure housewives out of their homes carrying unwanted scrap.

In the early days of the trade they really did collect rags and bones – the bones were sold to make bone china and the rags for paper – but in the latter half of the 20th century they came to collect any scrap metal or other items that they could sell on. They would often pay cash for items, only a few pence here and there, or offered exchanges, such as donkey stones, as they were called, for whitening doorsteps, but many people were happy using them as a way to clear out old junk that the binmen refused to take.

As the century drew to a close, households had become more focused on recycling, and most people had transport to take their scrap to local dumps and refuse centres. As a result, the trade has almost died out. But not quite. There are a few rag and bone men about, mostly still using a horse and cart (the slow progress they make gives people time to gather up items and take them outside). However, I suspect we will have seen the last of them in a few years' time.

Dodo Rating: 🐦🐦🐦🐦

Cars

Not all cars, obviously. Our roads are full of them, I know that. No, this entry is to mark the passing of the many makes of car that used to be everywhere on our roads, were often hugely popular, but which have ceased production and are gradually vanishing from the streets.

Take, for example, the Ford Sierra. It was one of the top ten most popular cars ever sold in Britain, with over 1.2 million machines on the roads, and ceased production in 1993. Almost anyone over the age of 35 could identify one immediately, but someone under 30 might struggle.

So here we commemorate some of the hugely popular motor vehicles, many of which we will have been driven in when we were younger, that have been parked in the scrapyard of history. See how many of them you can remember, and ask yourself when you last saw one on the open road.

Ford Anglia (1939–1967)
Citroen 2CV (1948–1990)
Morris Minor (1948–1971)
Ford Zephyr (1950–1972)
Triumph Herald (1959–1971)
Ford Cortina (1962–1982)
Hillman Imp (1963–1976)
Vauxhall Viva (1963–1979)
Datsun Sunny (1966–2004)
Ford Escort (1968–2003)
Ford Capri (1969–1986)
Morris Marina (1971–1980)
Ford Granada (1972–1994)
Austin Allegro (1973–1983)

Reliant Robin (1973–2002)
Toyota Starlet (1973–1999)
Vauxhall Cavalier (1975–1995)
Mini Metro (1980–1997)
Ford Sierra (1982–1993)
Austin Maestro (1983–1994)
Austin Montego (1984–1994)

Dodo Rating: 🐤🐤🐤🐤

Slam Door Trains

Allow me to set the scene.

My secondary school let pupils out at 3.30pm.

The train station was a three-minute walk away. Two minutes if you ran.

The train left the station at 3.32pm.

The moments after the home bell rang were, as you can probably imagine, utter chaos.

Dozens of scruffy boys, ties flailing in the wind, pegging it down the street in an attempt to catch the early train home. If you missed it, then you had to wait half an hour for the next one. Half an hour to a 12-year-old-boy is a lifetime, especially when he could be at home playing on his Vic 20.

With modern trains, we would have stood no chance. Push-button, centrally controlled electronic doors closing 30 seconds before departure would have kept us at bay.

But we didn't have modern trains back then (this was the early '80s). Instead, we had the slam door trains, carriages with individual doors, each with a handle you turned to open. The point being that they could be opened at any point during the journey, not just at the station.

So what happened was this – the faster runners would sprint ahead and make it to the station just as the train was pulling in. They would get on the train in normal fashion but leave the doors open.

The reasonably fit but not particularly sporty boys (which included me) would follow in their wake, making it into the station just as the train was supposed to leave. We'd usually be able to jump on at the open doors just as the guard was shouting at us to close them.

Then came the fun bit.

The weak, infirm, lovers of chocolate bars, lazy, and poorly shod would stagger to the station, out of breath and sweating, just as the train was leaving. The carriages were in motion, the train was on its way, the guard had shut his door and was busy lighting his fag for a quick puff before the next stop.

At this point we opened all the doors at the back of the train, ready for our less-athletic friends, or those with teachers who had not let them leave on time, to make ambitious, courageous, and foolhardy attempts to jump on.

Their legs would be going nine to the dozen, they would sometimes throw their bags ahead of them (a very risky strategy), and then they would make the leap of faith, ready for us to drag them on board. There were some casualties, of course, with people getting left behind and the occasional grazed knee, but it did make the journey home that little bit more exciting.

And the fun didn't stop there. The doors had slide-down windows and despite the warning not to stick your head out of them, we all pretty much did for most of the journey home. Of course, this meant dodgy half-eaten sandwiches (and often worse) lobbed out of the front windows in the hope of splatting some unsuspecting kid further down.

I have no idea why they no longer run such trains. No idea at all.

Dodo Rating: 🐥🐥🐥

Milk Bottle Deliveries

As recently as 20 years ago, most mornings would start with the electric hum of a milk float making slow and steady progress down the street, the clink and clank of bottles as they were carried by the milkman, and the sight of a pure white pint of milk on pretty much every doorstep on every street.

Today you will be hard pressed to find glass milk bottles in front of a house. You will rarely be caught behind a slow-moving float. You probably can't remember the last time you were woken by the cheerful (but slightly annoying) whistle of your milkman. Or the last note you wrote for him.

The daily milk delivery at the crack of dawn was a national institution. Red top, blue top, silver top, gold top, even the weird long-necked bottle of non-homogenised milk could be found on the doorstep. The classic image of a blue tit pecking away at the foil bottle top was a regular sight back then. As was the array of empties left at the end of the day ready for the milkman to collect, often with a rolled up note sticking out of the top with 'NO MILK TODAY' or 'ONE EXTRA PINT PLEASE'.

The big national dairies such as Unigate and Co-op would advertise on television (see the entry for Humphrey in a few pages' time) and their milkmen would sell lots more besides milk, but more on that shortly as well. They were all over the country, six days a week (no delivery on Sunday), and were part of the dawn chorus.

But sadly no more. There are still milkmen, and there are still door-to-door deliveries, but nowhere near the numbers there once were. A couple of years ago, during a fit of nostalgia, I signed up for a milk delivery after many years without one. It turned out that the milkman would only deliver every other day, and even then wasn't 100% reliable. I ended up cancelling after less than a month.

That sort of decline, and the simple fact that milk in cardboard and plastic cartons can be purchased from every corner shop, newsagent, and supermarket, means that the end of the milkman may be only a few years away.

This, when you think about it, is a bit odd. We are constantly being berated as an increasingly lazy nation, we have everything delivered nowadays – books, shopping, vegetable boxes, electronics – and yet the one thing that was traditionally always delivered to our door is something most of us don't want any more. Quite peculiar.

Dodo Rating: 🐥🐥🐥🐥

Fizzy Pop Deliveries

Your milkman didn't just deliver milk, of course; he could deliver eggs, butter, cheese, bread; and, most exciting of all, fizzy pop.

But we are not talking cans of Coca-Cola or 7up here; oh no, these were own-brand glass bottles of cherryade, orangeade, lime-ade, and, most special of all, cream soda.

Waking up on a Saturday morning to find a lukewarm bottle of brightly coloured pop on your doorstep was more exciting than you'd imagine. Sometimes the rich kids would have a veritable rainbow of fizziness outside the door, soon to send them into spasms of hyperactivity only cured in those days by a jolly good clout round the ear.

Life was so much simpler then.

Dodo Rating: 🐤🐤🐤🐤

Christmas Boxes

Boxing Day gets its name from the small earthenware boxes that the poor would use in medieval times to save for Christmas treats. They would smash these open and spend the contents on something special in the festive season.

This idea changed somewhat over the years, and became the name for gifts given to tradesmen on or around Christmas time. Households would put aside a few coins or a bottle of booze for the milkman, postman, and other regular callers, and hand them out during Christmas week.

The practice has pretty much died out in recent years. When I handed a bottle of wine to my postman a couple of years ago, he said it was the only gift he had received that year.

So why have we stopped rewarding those who deliver to our doorsteps, come rain or shine? Are we less generous than our parents and grandparents? Are times tougher? Are people less deserving?

I think the answer is quite different. We get fewer door-to-door callers, and those that do come are not always the same people. Think about it, how many of us still have a milkman delivering to our door? And when it comes to postmen and women, we used to have the same person delivering at about the same time every day. If we wanted to give the postman his Christmas box, we knew we could catch him at 7.15 on Christmas Eve morning (or whatever time he usually delivered). Mum would lie in wait with a pound note or a bottle of plonk, and hand it over with words of Christmas cheer and best wishes for the year ahead. Nowadays my mail can arrive any time from 7.00 in the morning till 4.00 in the afternoon, and I rarely have the same postman twice.

We no longer have friendly relationships with the people who deliver to our door – milkmen used to be notorious for knocking up bored housewives, but I bet that doesn't happen all that much any more, either – and, as a result, we don't feel the need to offer them a gift at Christmas. I think this is a shame, and is a tradition that I would love to see restored.

As would my postman.

Dodo Rating: 🐤🐤🐤

ON THE HIGH STREET

*Where we shopped, banked,
parked, and hung about ...*

Petrol Pump Attendants

You'd pull up at the petrol station in your Rover 3500, Ford Capri, or perhaps Austin Allegro [insert your own nostalgia-inducing make and model here], and onto the forecourt would waddle a chap in overalls.

'Fill her up,' you would cry cheerfully from behind the wheel. And fill her up he would, as well as checking the oil, water, and tyres, while he was at it.

You may find it hard to believe, but this was how *everyone* got their petrol until the onset of self-service stations in the 1970s. You didn't even have to get out of the car to pay. The attendant would take your money, pop back to his kiosk, and return with a fistful of change.

That, my friends, was proper customer service.

The idea of the petrol pump attendant actually harks back to a time before the garage forecourt, when fuel would be delivered to the homes of the privileged few who could afford to own a motor vehicle. It seemed natural for that personal service to extend to all customers when cars became more affordable and widely available.

One of the last attendants in the country, Dudley Oliver of Bentley's Garage in Exmouth, finally hung up his nozzle in 2010, not for lack of business, but rather because the ancient pumps were beginning to fall foul of health and safety laws, and would prove too costly to replace. The garage continues to trade for repairs and, in a nice touch, for free oil, water, and tyre checks, with Mr Oliver, kept on the payroll to valet cars.

So it isn't all bad news, although for one elderly lady customer it did truly mark the end: 'I've never had to put petrol in my car myself and I'm not going to start now.'

Dodo Rating: 🦤🦤🦤🦤🦤

Green Shield Stamps

Before the days of loyalty cards and Nectar points, we had Green Shield Stamps. These were small, about the size of a postage stamp, and dispensed from machines at the tills of many supermarkets, petrol stations, and corner shops. Customers collected them and stuck them into books; completed books could then be traded in for items of differing value from a catalogue, or from one of the many Green Shield Stamp catalogue shops.

You had to collect loads of the buggers to be able to get hold of anything remotely worthwhile, but that didn't stop the little green things proliferating across the '60s and '70s.

You would need to spend a little over £32 to fill one book. That was a lot of money in those days, equivalent to over £350 today. That one book, which would have taken you considerable time to fill, could be exchanged for items such as a mouth organ or a brush and comb set.

More serious collectors, those who stacked up piles of books, could go for rather grander fare. In the 1960s, 33¼ books would get you a Kenwood Chef, an item many kitchens would have been proud to have. Of course, the amount of money you would have to spend to obtain said food mixer was about the price of a small car. Although, to be fair, if you were spending the money on your weekly shop and petrol anyway, it was just a case of being patient and licking lots of stamps.

The company was founded in 1958 by Richard Tompkins, who adapted an idea from the United States to fit the British and Irish markets. It was hugely successful for nearly two decades, and there were many imitators, including S&H Pink Stamps, Yellow Stamps, Blue Star, and Happy Clubs. At one point in the early '60s there was even a 'Stamp War' when Fine Fare supermarkets started offering the Pink Stamps, and Tesco countered by giving away Green Shield Stamps for the first time.

The business came a cropper in the late-'70s, when competition between supermarkets hit new heights, and customers were more interested in cheap produce than collecting stamps. When Tesco pulled out of the scheme in 1977, the writing was on the wall for the little green shield.

The company limped on until 1983, when it stopped issuing stamps altogether. There was an attempt to reinvent the scheme in the late '80s, but by 1991 the Green Shield Stamp company was no more.

It does live on, however, in some form at least. The Green Shield Stamp catalogue shops were rebranded as Argos in 1973, and continue trading to this day, with people actually paying cash for items that previous generations would get for free after purchasing 2,500 packets of fish fingers over 13 years, or something like that.

And, of course, the concept was brought up to date in recent years by the introduction of loyalty cards, air miles, and Nectar points.

Dodo Rating:

High Street Names

This is a roll call of chains and shops that were once on every high street in the country, but are now no longer with us. How many did you use to shop in?

Abbey National, ABC Cinemas, Alfred Marks, Andy's Records, Anglian Building Society, Athena, Bejam, Bradford & Bingley, Brentford Nylons, C&A, Canon Cinemas, Chelsea Girl, Concept Man, Courts, Curtess, Deep Pan Pizza Co., DER, Dewhursts, DH Evans, Dickens & Jones, Dillons, Dixons, Dominics Wine Merchants, Elf, Etam, Fina, Fine Fare, Fosters, Freeman, Hardy & Willis, Gateway, Golden Egg Restaurants, Granada, Happy Eater, Home & Colonial, International, James Thin, John Menzies, Lilley & Skinner, Liptons, Littlewoods, Lyons Cafés, MFI, Midland Bank, Mister Byrite, MVC, NafNaf, National Provincial Bank, Ottakars, Our Price, Payless, Pizzaland, Pollards, Presto, Principles, Radio Rentals, Ratners, Rediffusion, Richard Shops, Rumbelows, Safeway, Savacentre, Saxone, Swan & Edgar, Tandy, Texas Homecare, The Electricity Shop, The Gas Shop, Thresher, Timothy Whites, Tower Records, Unwins, VG, Victoria Wine, Wavy Line, Woolwich, Woolworths, World of Leather.

These are just a small selection of well-known names that have gone bust, been rebranded or taken over, or just slowly faded away over the past couple of decades. Now let's have a closer look at the stories behind the demise of some of these.

Dodo Rating: 🐤🐤🐤🐤🐤

Woolworths

In almost every town in the UK there remains a Woolworths-sized hole, often in a very real and physical sense.

The company went bust in 2009, with the loss of over 800 stores and 27,000 jobs. At its peak, there were over 1,100 Woolworths shops across the UK.

Originally an American company founded by F.W. Woolworth, the tycoon was proud of his English heritage and embarked upon a controversial transatlantic expansion programme, opening his first UK store in Liverpool in 1909, much against the advice of many of his business partners.

His 'nickel and dime' store concept translated well to the British market, and the range of household goods at affordable prices was a considerable success, allowing him to expand across the country, hitting the peak of store numbers in the 1960s.

The 'wonder of Woolies', as an old advertising campaign went, became a national institution, and there was hardly a high street in the land that didn't have a branch with its readily identifiable logo hanging above the door.

Over the decades since the stores first opened, the chain experimented with many different product lines but always kept affordable homeware at the heart of its offer. These were joined by music and video (for many years Woolworths was the leading entertainment retailer in the country), clothing (the Ladybird range for kids), restaurants (the place to go if you were a pensioner in search of a good fry-up), toys (the Chad Valley label), and, most importantly of all, pic 'n' mix sweets.

Everyone at some point in their lives would have shopped in a branch of Woolworths, most people doing so several times a month. They were part of the fabric of our society.

So, what went wrong?

Well, in the early '80s the American parent company sold the UK stores to the Kingfisher Group and, while the chain continued to thrive under new ownership, it also expanded into other areas, including book and CD distribution. Supermarkets were increasingly offering similar ranges, and customers were picking up the products they'd normally buy from Woolworths while doing their weekly grocery shop. Perhaps the biggest single impact was the digital revolution in music. The company was a major player in CD sales, but in a few short years the market collapsed and management struggled to find a way to fill the gap. Whereas its closest rival in this area, HMV, was able to expand into DVD box sets, computer games, and entertainment hardware, Woolworths didn't manage to pull the punters in for the same product.

Whatever the reason, by the late 2000s they were really struggling and, seemingly overnight, the whole chain collapsed. Woolworths was placed into administration in November 2008, and the final branch closed in January 2009.

Ironically, the closing-down sales across the stores brought the company's best trading days ever, with tens of millions of pounds being spent every day by customers keen to pick up a bargain (some lines were reduced by 90%), or perhaps just wanting to bid farewell to a shop that had been there all of their lives. Most high streets were left with a big gap to fill, and over 300 Woolworths branches remained empty more than two years later.

Many of the old sites have been snapped up by other retailers, and a few have even been bought by ex-Woolworths staff. A former employee in Dorchester re-opened her branch as Wellworths, just two months after it closed down. It is still doing well. The Woolworths name itself is now used to front an online retail business.

Businesses go bust all the time, well-known names are merged, taken over, or bought out, but it is rare for the whole nation to mourn their loss. We all grew up with Woolworths. We bought our first LPs there. Flirted with our first girlfriends or boyfriends over the counter. We worked there. We rotted our teeth on the pic 'n' mix. We won a few quid on the lottery. We picked up our copy of *Heat* magazine. We trod its linoleum aisles, along with the rest of the nation.

And now it is no more. It is sorely missed.

Dodo Rating: 🐦🐦🐦🐦

Midland Bank

The Midland Bank was founded as the Birmingham and Midland Bank in 1836, adopting its shorter name in 1923. It became the largest deposit bank in the world, and, throughout the last century, was a fixture of the high street in nearly every town in the UK.

Then it was taken over by HSBC, never to be heard of again.

Mergers and acquisitions take place all the time in the world of high finance, so this did not necessarily come as a surprise, but it is unusual for such an established institution to vanish completely.

People tend to have a lifelong relationship with their bank. They perhaps open an account as a child, somewhere to put their birthday and Christmas money, receiving their first cashpoint card as a teenager, before graduating to a 'grown-up' account. They get a job and see their monthly salary paid in, they take a loan for their first car, buy a house, get a mortgage, store their savings. All with the same bank.

So when their trusted bank, where they have placed their money all their lives, is absorbed into another company, it is a big deal, and worthy of note.

Even if you didn't bank with Midland, you will remember their logo – a golden griffin surrounded by a circle of coins – and their slogan, 'the listening bank'. You would have seen them in TV adverts, on billboards, and illuminated outside their branches. They really were everywhere.

And now they are nowhere, replaced by, to give them their full name, the Hong Kong and Shanghai Banking Corporation.

Not quite the same, is it?

Dodo Rating: 🐦🐦🐦🐦🐦

C&A

Of course, not all chains that have vanished from our high streets have disappeared from the face of the earth completely. C&A, purveyors of reasonably priced clothes for the discerning man and woman about town, closed down their UK stores in 2001, in the face of competition from supermarkets and other discount designer chains, but across Europe they continue to be a major player.

So much so that Beyoncé (she who would have preferred you to put a ring on it) has her own clothing line in conjunction with the chain.

In the UK, brands such as Clockhouse, Palomino, and Yessica made them popular with both sexes and they were often the store that mothers didn't mind their children buying clothes from – their ranges being cheap and relatively fashionable. Their 'Man at C&A' advertising campaign offered smart trousers and shirts to the impressionable teenager intent on wowing the girl at the forthcoming school disco. They were also the go-to store for cheap salopettes for school skiing trips.

The gap left by the departure of C&A was quickly filled by Primark, New Look, Matalan, and the like, so you wouldn't really know they were ever here.

Unless, that is, you remember purchasing your first pair of waffled trousers there in 1981. As many of us do.

Dodo Rating: 🐦🐦

Our Price

At its peak, Our Price was the second biggest music retailer in the country behind Woolworths (before then there was a time when Woolies, WH Smith, and Boots were the three largest, can you imagine?!), with over 300 stores across the country. Originally set up as a cassette specialist, the loyalty to the format continued for much of its existence, with plenty of space given over to tapes even when they were clearly on the way out.

Founded in 1972, the chain went through the hands of several owners, most notably WH Smith, who bought it in 1986, but they each managed to maintain the fairly ramshackle indie feel, helped by the wire rack displays and handwritten header cards. There was an Our Price in almost every major town, and many music lovers aged 30+ will have an LP, cassette, or CD somewhere in their collection that still bears an Our Price sticker.

During the mid- to late-'80s, Our Price faced stiff competition from the HMV chain, and the larger, bolder, and more fashionable newcomer soon overtook its smaller rival. This marked the beginning of the end. A period of rebranding as Virgin stores did nothing to reverse its fortunes and the chain finally went under in early 2004, with all the stock being sold to Oxfam.

Our Price still exists in two incarnations, however. There is an online company supplying music memorabilia to charities, and there is also an original Our Price store sitting empty in Wolverhampton city centre. Several years after closure, and no one has taken over the site.

I bet there is a copy of *Now That's What I Call Music Vol. 23* in there somewhere.

On cassette, obviously.

Dodo Rating: 🦤🦤🦤🦤

Athena

Athena epitomised the 1980s in the same way that the Raleigh Chopper summed up the 1970s. Its product range of reproduction art prints, calendars, and novelty items was perfect for the decade that style forgot, but with '80s fashion and music making a determined comeback, is there time for Athena to stage a revival?

It started out as an art shop in the early '60s, but its most famous incarnation was born out of a corporate takeover and expansion programme that saw it grow to 60 stores nationwide.

Classic Athena products included *L'Enfant*, a black and white photograph of a male model holding a small baby, and the iconic *Tennis Girl* poster (you know, the one with the bare arse).

The company collapsed in 1995 and only survives through seven branches that managed to stay open following administration.

Dodo Rating: 🐦🐦🐦🐦

Television Rental Shops

In the early days of television, very few people actually bought one. They were bloody expensive. Instead, people rented them from electrical stores and chains such as Radio Rentals, Rediffusion, or Rumbelows (there must have been some law that meant they had to begin with the letter R). For a small amount each week you could have a brand-spanking-new Bush or Ferguson sitting in the corner of your living room on which you could watch the wrestling, or *One Man and his Dog*, perhaps. When your rental period expired, you could upgrade to a new model.

Rental companies, who could also let you have anything from a fridge-freezer to a video recorder, experienced a massive slump in business in the 1990s when technology became cheaper and consumers, in the main, opted to buy their entertainment systems outright. It became very rare to see a rental shop on the high street.

This was a real problem for many married men for whom a TV rental store window display was the only way to catch up on the football scores while out shopping with the wife on a Saturday afternoon.

We may be about to come full circle, however. The speed at which televisual technology is advancing means that your £2,000 42" HD LCD monitor is pretty much out of date the moment you buy it. People are coming back round to the idea of shelling out a few quid a week in return for a cutting edge TV which they can exchange for a bigger, better, and newer one at the end of a year.

Husbands, your weekend shopping trips may not be a trauma for much longer.

Dodo Rating: 🐥🐥🐥🐥

Fish and Chips Wrapped in Newspaper

Until the middle of the 1980s, anything you ordered from your local fish and chip shop would come wrapped in newspaper. The practice was outlawed by those party poopers at Health and Safety for fear that ingesting newsprint would be bad for our health.

Now, I have a few things to say about that.

Firstly, the fish and chips were never actually placed directly into newspaper. There was usually some sort of greaseproof lining or paper bag between the grub and the headlines, so it was very unlikely that any ink would get on the chips.

And, even if it did, there is absolutely no research suggesting that it was bad for your health anyway.

But my biggest issue is with the replacement. Instead of newspapers, we now have cardboard cones printed with fake newspaper headlines, or polystyrene trays, and they are both pants.

And then there is the old saying, usually spoken by a politician or celebrity who has just taken a thumping from the press, that 'today's headlines are tomorrow's chip wrappers', which just doesn't make sense any more, however true the sentiment may be.

Dodo Rating:

Keeping CDs Behind the Counter

They were called masterbags. Cardboard sleeves that record stores kept behind the counter which held the popular CDs, tapes, and LPs of the time.

The covers and cases were out on the shop floor. Empty.

You, the customer, would select your copy of *Stars* by Simply Red on CD, or *Circus* by Erasure on cassette, take the case up to the counter, and the dodgy looking bloke at the till would vanish amidst a network of shelves and cubby holes to locate the innards for you, quietly muttering to himself about your shite taste in music.

I know, I was that dodgy-looking bloke.

Working in record shops in the '80s and '90s meant a great deal of rooting around in a sea of masterbags to find the customer's selection. This was usually a relatively simple process with most CDs, which were filed in alphabetical order by artist (ignoring any instances of The or A in the band name, unless the band name was The The, in which case you were best not ignoring it, to be honest). The name being written on the edge of the cardboard sleeve made it easy to flick through.

It got more complicated when it came to cassettes or classical CDs, which were placed in order of price and catalogue number.

Of course, any system like this relies on librarian-like discipline when it comes to the storage and filing of items. But these were shops managed and staffed by 20-something rock music fans. And teenage Saturday staff.

Mistakes did happen.

When you couldn't find a particular item among the sea of cardboard, you would call upon one of your colleagues to help out. Some of these people had been working there for a while and knew their way around the musical alphabet, and often knew the classic misfiling – bands might have been misread as artist names, so Rolling Stones had ended up under S – but if that failed, then you had no option but to call out Dave from the stockroom.

Dave was the bloke in charge of re-ordering the stock, and the man who wrote out all of the masterbags. These were his babies. He knew where they were. He didn't, however, much like the idea of coming out onto the shop floor, so you called on him at your own risk. If you timed it for just after his 11am coffee then you were probably OK.

Meanwhile, as all of this was going on, a huge queue was developing, with people eager to buy Adamski's 'Killer' on 12" single, or keen to return a defective copy of *Woodface* by Crowded House ('I tried rewinding it with a pencil, but it wouldn't work').

We now live in a time of security tags, and record stores happily leave the stock intact when it goes onto the shop floor. This reduces the time taken at the till, which would be fine if it wasn't then used to try to get you to join the loyalty card scheme, or to buy a copy of the new Justin Bieber CD for only £3.99, seeing as you have already spent £20 ('I'd rather have it inserted anally, thank you').

But that's progress for you.

Dodo Rating: 🐦🐦🐦🐦🐦

Half-day Closing

If you wanted to buy a loaf of bread after 1pm on a Wednesday where I grew up, you were buggered. The same would have been the case throughout the country. The day might differ from place to place, but everywhere had its half-day closing. Pretty much every shop on the high street would be closed, with the exception of the post office. It would be proper tumbleweed territory come five past one.

The reason for bringing down the shutters at lunchtime one day a week was pretty simple: shopkeepers worked Monday to Saturday with only Sunday off. At least, that was the case until pressure mounted, and legislation was brought in to give workers an additional half-day's holiday each week. Some individual town and village councils had introduced the rule in the late 19th century, but it wasn't until the Shops Act in 1911 that it became enshrined in law.

Wednesday was usually the day set aside for early closing because it was conveniently located slap bang in the middle of the week. But this wasn't the same everywhere, with Thursdays and Mondays often put to the same purpose. This could lead to great confusion when people were visiting from one town to another.

Looking back now in our time of 24-hour shopping and the changes in Sunday trading laws, this whole half-day closing malarkey seems awfully quaint and Olde English, but it was fairly common right up until the mid-1980s. It created a haven of peace and quiet in the centre of every town in the country, and there was a lot to be said for that.

Nowadays you won't find any town, or even village, which observes half-day closing traditions, but you can still come across the odd shop here and there, often owned by elderly proprietors, who insist on closing at midday on a Wednesday. And long may they do so.

Dodo Rating: 🐤🐤🐤🐤

Record Tokens

If you are aged 40 or over, then there is a strong chance that somewhere in your house – at the bottom of the junk drawer, in an old shoebox under the bed, tucked away in the attic – there can still be found a record token.

An unused, out-of-date, and now completely worthless record token.

The principle was simple. Anyone could buy a record token from any music store and send it, using the free gift card it came with, to anyone else in the country. That person could then redeem the voucher in their own local record shop.

Rather neat.

The beauty of this system was that it enabled wizened old grannies with smelly hallways to give their unappreciative grandsons a birthday gift that was actually of some use. Rather than a pair of socks. Or a Ladybird book about reservoirs.

The scheme was administered by EMI and supported by all record shops, from the smallest specialist independent, to the big chains like WH Smith, HMV, and Boots (hands up if you remember Boots selling records). It spread the sales around. The token may have been purchased in Smiths in Sheffield, but was spent in Fives in Rayleigh. Or vice versa. For many people, their first ever record purchase was facilitated by a £3 record token. Or £5. Or £10. Depending what decade you grew up in.

The tokens themselves were small oblong pieces of card, in different colours for each denomination. The bottom portion was licked like a stamp by the sales assistant and stuck into a greetings card – you often had a choice of cards, all shite – when you bought them. When they were redeemed at the other end, the tokens were ripped across a perforation and popped into the till.

The system worked perfectly well for decades, until WH Smith introduced its own tokens. Other retailers followed suit and, over time, only the independents sold the EMI ones. The writing was on the wall, and they had vanished by the end of the 20th century.

Apart from the £5 token lying at the bottom of your wardrobe, of course.

If you added up all these lost, misplaced, ignored, and unused tokens, I reckon you'd have enough money to fill the current finance deficit. Just a guess, but try to prove me wrong.

Dodo Rating: 🐤🐤🐤🐤

AT SCHOOL

*Where we learnt, got into trouble,
and grazed our knees …*

Blackboards

Have you been into a school recently?

Where have all the blackboards gone?

Seriously, it is all whiteboards and computer projector screens and marker pens nowadays. No blackboards. No chalk. All very modern.

I can remember two types of blackboard from my school days. One, the most common, was the fixed blackboard at the end of the classroom, next to the teacher's desk. This was the focal point of all lessons. It was where the spelling list went up, where the sums were displayed, where whole passages were written for us to copy out. There was usually some sort of ledge or shelf that held the chalk and duster. It was like a massive black window.

And then there was the rolling blackboard, the slightly more portable version. Usually on wheels, it was more portrait than landscape, and had a reel of coated material stretched across it so that it could be rolled down as it was used, a bit like a revolving hand towel in a public toilet. It meant the teacher could move on to a fresh, blank area when he or she had used up the space in front of them, but also allowed for a big reveal. The name of a special project, or the answer to a puzzle that the kids had been working on, could be written up and then rolled round to the other side, ready to be pulled down on cue.

The rolling blackboard still had to be cleaned, but it did give you a bit of time with the duster between sessions. It also allowed the pupils to draw a penis or write 'Mrs Jones is smelly' while the teacher was out, roll the blackboard down, and then convulse in spasms of anticipation as they waited for it to come round again. Along with the inevitable detention.

Of course, blackboards were rarely actually black. They very quickly became grey, coated as they were with layers of chalk dust.

All the blackboard duster did was spread that dust around, really, although it was still a sought-after job for the kids in the class, teachers often handing out the task to the 'person who is sitting most still and quiet'.

But the best job of all was when you were asked to clean the blackboard with a wet cloth. This opportunity only came round once a week or so, but was the chance to get the blackboard back to its original glory. All traces of chalk were gone and, for a few brief moments, it looked pristine, unblemished. It was a thing of beauty. And then the teacher would start writing on it again.

This, in itself, was quite an art form. Have you ever tried writing with a new piece of chalk on a blackboard? It is bloody difficult, and especially hard to have anything remotely resembling neat handwriting while doing so. I guess this is now a dying art, writing on a whiteboard with a felt-tip is much easier.

As the blackboard vanishes off into the past with a puff of chalk dust, so does the origin of the phrase 'Like fingernails down a blackboard'. We all know what that means, and some of us will have goosebumps at the very thought, but do our children? And will our children's children?

Another classic image lost in the march of progress.

Dodo Rating:

Blackboard Rubbers

With the death of the blackboard comes that of the blackboard rubber.

Yes, I know that whiteboards also have rubbers, but they don't leave a comet trail of chalk dust as they fly towards the head of an unsuspecting child who is busy nattering to his best mate about the fact that he can see Jessica Hunter's knickers.

This is almost as much fun as the sound it makes as it connects with said boy's head and showers his school blazer with chalk.

Not that teachers are allowed to do that sort of thing any more, more's the pity.

Dodo Rating: 🐦🐦🐦🐦

Antiseptic in the Playground

OK, this is what used to happen.

You'd be playing British Bulldog in the playground, get splatted by the fat kid in the class above you, and end up with a torn trouser leg and a grazed knee full of grit and dirt.

Holding in the tears, you would hobble over to the dinner lady on duty, present her with your mortal wound, and she would take you to her medical box which contained only three items:

- some cotton wool
- a box of plasters
- a bottle of mysterious liquid

She would then proceed to douse the cotton wool with the mysterious liquid, press it against your knee, tell you to stop being a big baby (as you experienced pain greater than childbirth), and then plonk a plaster over the top and send you on your way.

Nowadays, when a child falls over in the playground, parents get a letter a little something like this:

Dear Mr and Mrs Stack,

Your son/daughter received an injury at school today. The graze was treated with distilled water. No medication was given to your child.

If you have any questions regarding the incident, please do not hesitate to call us.

Yours sincerely,

The Headmistress

ps Please do not sue us.

Dodo Rating: 🐦🐦🐦🐦🐦

Calculator Watches

It is hard to believe now, in a world in which school playgrounds are awash with iPods, mobile phones, Nintendo 3DS, and all manner of other devices, but the most impressive thing a kid could bring into school in the 1970s was a calculator watch.

That is partly because it was one of the few things you were allowed to bring in. OK, so none of those other things were invented then, but these were the early days of portable (albeit very basic) electronic games, and pretty much every school in the land forbade pupils to use them there.

A calculator watch, on the other hand (pun noted, but not intended), was perfectly acceptable. It was, after all, an educational item, although woe betide any child foolish enough to wear one during a maths exam.

Casio was the manufacturer that really went to town on calculator watches, producing a wide variety of versions, each more swanky and with more scientific functions than the last.

Not that many people used their watches for such elaborate equations. They were all too busy with the hilarious result of the sum 6,922,251 x 8.

Dodo Rating: 🐦🐦🐦🐦

Satchels

Whatever happed to satchels? We all used to have them. Slung over the shoulder with just enough room for your schoolbooks, a Spam sandwich, and a Club biscuit, plus a few chewed stubby pencils.

I suppose they were replaced by sports bags with swooshes or three stripes, and designer handbags from knockoff stalls down the market.

A shame, really; I still think they are rather cool. Indiana Jones had one, you know.

Dodo Rating: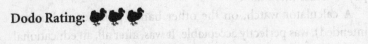

78

Ice Cream Bricks

Please tell me I am not the only person who remembers these. I have been asking around, and cannot find anyone who recollects them. I am not talking about the blocks of ice cream you can buy in most supermarkets – they are still (thank the Lord!) readily available, and only a quick slice with a sharp knife away from forming the perfect dessert – no, I mean the individual rectangular cuboid of vanilla ice cream that slotted into cones with square holes.

I've confused you now, haven't I? Allow me to elaborate.

At my primary school summer fête there used to be an ice cream stall run by the dinner ladies. They had individual blocks of ice cream, about the size of two Weetabix sellotaped together, but with square corners, wrapped in paper. They also had stacks of wafer cones that had rectangular tops rather than the traditional round ones. When you bought your ice cream cone – they were 10p in my day, but this was a long time ago – they unwrapped a bit of the block, shoved it in the hole, finished unwrapping, and handed it over.

It was the ideal way to serve hundreds of kids without needing a scoop, a tub of hot water, or getting your hands dirty.

Come to think of it, I seem to recall that we would get served these treats once or twice a year at school dinners. I am guessing this was probably the first Monday after the fête!

I haven't seen any of these rectangular beauties for a good 30 years. I wonder if they still exist?*

Dodo Rating: 🐤🐤🐤🐤

---

* **Update:** *I have received a few emails from readers who also remember these semi-frozen treats, so it is't just me.*

Corporal Punishment

This was on its way out when I was a lad back in the '70s, but it was only eradicated from all British schools as recently as 2003 (where the last private schools in Northern Ireland finally stopped the practice). It was banned in state schools in 1987. The year I left. Coincidence? I think not.

In olden times, the weapon of choice for headmasters and teachers was the cane, a whippy piece of bamboo or similar wood, that would administer a good whack and a mighty sting to whichever part of the body it was applied to with force. To this day, the classic image of a posh schoolboy hiding a book down his trousers to deaden the pain of six of the best is well known to all.

But it wasn't just the cane, the slipper was also a common punishment implement, presumably because the flexible sole gave it a bit of heft. I can recall my PE teacher using an old trainer to spank the kids who forgot their kit. The fact that he used to administer this punishment in the showers probably harmed his reputation more than it acted as a deterrent.

Some teachers, such as my history teacher Mr Milne, were more creative with their punishments. He would stand behind the offending boy and pick him up by the little straggly bits of hair by the ears; if you didn't manage to stand up in time with him, then it was agony.

But hilarious to the rest of the class.

And that was the thing. Apart from some extreme cases of proper cruelty, I don't think most kids minded corporal punishment. It added some excitement to school life. Getting caught doing something wrong got you a rap over the knuckles or a blackboard rubber hurled at you across the room, and that made it more risky, gave it an edge.

I know I sound like a real old fogey, but discipline in schools now is a genuine problem; there must be some connection between this and the fact that a teacher can no longer give someone a whack. If my son came home from school and told me he'd had a clip round the ear for being cheeky, I'd say it served him right. Many other parents would sue, the teacher would be suspended, and it would be front-page news.

So, while I am not mourning the passing of a proper bare-arsed caning, I do think it is a shame, for both teachers and pupils, that the war of Us v. Them isn't made that little bit more dangerous by the allowance of a tiny amount of violence from the grown-ups.

Dodo Rating: 🐤🐤🐤🐤🐤

Bulldog

That's what we used to call it, anyway. It is also known as British Bulldog, Bullrush, or numerous variations thereof. It is a school playground game that has been banned (or, at least, frowned on) by many head teachers because of risk of injury*.

Here are the rules, such as they were:

- A bunch of kids, the more the merrier, stand at one end of the playground.
- One child is elected to be the Bulldog. He or she stands in the middle of the playground.
- On the cry of 'Go', the mass of kids have to run from one side of the playground to the other, avoiding the Bulldog.
- The Bulldog has to catch one or more of the players as they rush by.
- A simple tag will not suffice; they actually have to wrestle their opponent to the ground or otherwise incapacitate them.
- Once captured, a player becomes a Bulldog and stays in the centre.
- When a 'run' has been completed – i.e. all the players have reached the other side – the whole thing starts again with players running back the other way.
- Repeat until there is only one player left, the rest being Bulldogs.
- Then, commence the Glory Run.

The Glory Run was the stuff of legends. Only one player remained standing at the end of the playground. Facing them were 10, 20, 30,

---

* For which read: 'fear of getting sued because little Johnny has grazed his knee'.

or more Bulldogs, all scenting blood. Everyone knew that the last man standing had no hope; it simply wasn't possible to get past that many Bulldogs.

But that didn't stop you trying. For a few fleeting seconds you thought you could do it, become the first person to survive the Glory Run. You had already won the game, now was the time for immortality.

You took a deep breath.

Glanced around quickly, desperately looking for a gap.

And legged it as fast as you could.

Chances are you came to, a few minutes later, at the bottom of a pile of Bulldogs. Defeated, but proud.

Of course, this was a full-contact sport and lots of people got hurt. Some of you reading this will have bad memories of Bulldog, and perhaps rightly so. It was dangerous. It was foolhardy. It was irresponsible and a bit silly.

But that was sort of the point.

Dodo Rating: 🦃🦃🦃🦃

Schools' Programmes
Countdown Clock

Before the days of video recorders and DVDs, the BBC and ITV used to show a range of educational programmes for schools in the late morning and early afternoon. These would cover all manner of topics from maths to English, science to computing, foreign languages to history.

If you were a school with only one television set, your teacher would lead you from your classroom to the hall, where you would sit down on the floor, or on benches, waiting for your programme to start.

Some of these programmes are well remembered to this day, such as *Look and Read* with Wordy, the disembodied head who would educate us through songs and short animations, or *How We Used To Live*, a dramatic account of the olden days. Others have faded away to be forgotten forever.

But the thing that no one will forget is the countdown clock. The schools programmes usually had a 5- to 10-minute gap between shows, presumably to allow schools to get shot of one class and bring another in, and that space was filled with an analogue clock counting down to the start of the next programme.

With two or three minutes to go, the benches would be a flurry of shuffling, pinching, punching, and kicking, as kids jostled for the best place – ideally out of sight of the teacher and not behind the kid with the massive afro.

With one minute to go, the teacher would inevitably yell at everyone to sit still.

And with ten seconds to go, the whole class would shout out the countdown.

10 ... 9 ... 8 ... 7 ... 6 ... 5 ... 4 ... 3 ... 2 ... 1!

In the 1970s, that was about as exciting as school got, I can assure you.

As the 1980s dragged on, the afternoons became a time for more traditional programming, and schools programmes started to be shifted to the evening or early morning, with schools being encouraged to record them on video to show during the day. In fact, a wide range of such shows is still aired in the early hours on the BBC, and are well worth viewing if you want to brush up on your Spanish or square roots!

Dodo Rating: 🐤🐤🐤🐤🐤

ON TELEVISION
AND RADIO

That we wasted hours in front of …

Answers on a Postcard

No children's show of the '70s, '80s, or even '90s, would have been complete without a competition to which the only way to enter would be to write an answer on a postcard and send it in to the studio.

Nowadays, of course, the BBC doesn't run competitions anymore after a series of 'scandals' revealed that some of them were rigged, and commercial channels have expensive phone and text quiz questions that are so mind-numbingly easy that it is an insult to the intelligence to actually pick up a phone and answer them. Here is an actual question that I saw on a TV show recently:

What nationality is the actor Tom Hanks?
a) Irish
b) Russian
c) American
d) French

There then follows about five paragraphs of small print along the lines of:

Calls will cost £1.50 from a landline but calls from a mobile will cost so much more that you will have to go without Heat magazine and fake tan for a month when your bill comes through and you realise how much you have pissed away on a stupid quiz that you stand little to no chance of winning. Lines close at 3pm but we'll still leave the lines open so we can fleece you for more money and, let's face it, if you do call after, then you deserve to be robbed. If anyone phones in and answers A, B, or D, then we will immediately send social services round to your house and remove your children. Judges' decision is final. Now, quick, put the phone

down and start watching again; we have an item about a girl
who crocheted a life-size model of her father in the hope that it
would bring her parents back together.

See? It's all a bit shit, really, isn't it?

I much preferred the transparent bin stuffed full of postcards from which Alvin Stardust or Zammo from *Grange Hill* would select the winner of a signed Five Star 12" single. Simpler times, but not without their own controversy. Some people would send in ridiculous oversized postcards in the hope that they would stand out, others went for bright colours or other blatantly cheating tactics, but OfCom never called for an inquiry when one of these were pulled out, did they? Oh no.

And to think, that autographed Adam and the Ants drum skin could have been mine if it wasn't for some bastard sending his answer in on a card shaped like a giant ant.

Dodo Rating:

Buzby

That bloody Russian meerkat wasn't the first star of a TV commercial to become a household name and spawn a successful range of merchandise. Oh no. Thirty-five years earlier, British Telecom (or Post Office Telecommunications, as it was then known) used a yellow cartoon bird to front its 'Make someone happy with a phone call' campaign.

Voiced by Bernard Cribbins, who was also the narrator of popular children's TV show *The Wombles* and a regular on *Jackanory*, Buzby became a big hit with the general public, especially kids, and you could buy books, toys, T-shirts, and badges. He even had his own comic strip.

But where is he now? Eh? Gone and pretty much forgotten, that's where.

Aleksandr Orlov had better watch out. He may end up going the same way.

Dodo Rating: 🐦🐦🐦🐦🐦

Humphrey

'Watch out, watch out, there's a Humphrey about!'

It was a stroke of advertising genius. In the 1970s, Unigate Dairies launched a campaign featuring an invisible creature who stole milk from celebrities – Rod Hull, Frank Muir, Arthur Mullard, and so on – using a very long red and white straw. The subliminal message, such as it was, presumably being to encourage kids to drink up their milk before Humphrey got it.

Whether the idea of a mysterious stranger sneaking up on kids while they were tucking into a glass of milk would pass muster with today's child safety-obsessed media is a matter for debate. At the time, everyone loved it.

There was even a range of merchandise you could purchase from your milkman, including mugs, T-shirts, hats, badges, and stickers, some of which crop up on eBay from time to time and fetch a fair few bob.

Although Humphrey himself has not been sighted for over 30 years, he was, as we have established, a master of disguise, so he could still be walking among us, for all we know.

Best keep a close eye on your pinta.

Dodo Rating: 🐤🐤🐤🐤🐤

Grandstand

Grandstand was the BBC's flagship sports programme, and was one of the longest-running television shows in history, airing across six decades from, 1958 to 2007.

During that time, the show covered 23 summer and winter Olympic Games, 13 Commonwealth Games, broadcast the first ever live hole-in-one at a golf tournament (Tony Jacklin in the 1967 Dunlop Masters), the first televised streaker (a 1974 England rugby match), and was also live on the scene for two of British sport's most tragic events, the Bradford City fire and the Hillsborough disaster. It also showed the 1966 World Cup Final and drew in an audience of over 27 million people.

Despite running for over 3,000 editions, *Grandstand* only ever had four main presenters (supplemented by many guest presenters over the years). These were David Coleman, Frank Bough, Des Lynam, and Steve Rider, with Des becoming an unlikely sex symbol during his tenure. I met Des once; he called me a scruffy bastard.

For nearly 20 years (1968 to 1985), *Grandstand* ran head to head against its ITV rival *World of Sport* but there was very little cross-over, apart from a bit of horse racing and football, between the two schedules. While ITV favoured wrestling and angling, the BBC was a bit more upmarket, with skiing, horse jumping, and athletics.

In its later years *Grandstand* relied less on a studio presenter and more on live outside broadcasts with commentators and experts at each event. This, coupled with the decision to carve off *Football Focus* and *Final Score* into separate programmes, led to the show being cancelled, with the last episode broadcast on 27 January 2007.

Dodo Rating:

World of Sport

It's Saturday, it's half past twelve, and the opening bars of a familiar theme tune burst through the television speaker as a fleet of light aircraft trail three words behind them.

Those words are, of course, WORLD, OF, and SPORT.

For the rest of Saturday afternoon the show would broadcast a range of sports, from bowls to wrestling, to a grateful nation. It was ITV's answer to BBC's hugely popular *Grandstand*, and, although the two shows were in competition, they rarely clashed in terms of the sports being shown. The more prim and proper BBC was not interested in the shenanigans of Giant Haystacks and Big Daddy, or niche sports such as speedway and ten-pin bowling, and was content to let ITV dabble in such things.

The truth was, of course, that the BBC owned the rights to pretty most all the major sporting events, and ITV, through *World of Sport*, was forced to cover specialist interest sports around a central spine of football scores and horse racing.

To give you an idea of a typical *World of Sport* broadcast, here is the actual listing from 8 November 1980:

12.35 ON THE BALL
Ian St John presents a round-up of this week's European action, where Britain's leading clubs have been striving to achieve further success. Plus features, analysis, and news.

1.00 INTERNATIONAL SPORTS SPECIAL – 1
The Angling Times Champion of Champions
from Weirwood Reservoir, Sussex
Ace anglers compete for a £750 first prize in this first event staged for television. Weirwood Reservoir, near East Grinstead, holds large quantities of 2-lb-plus roach, so an exceptional

winning weight is possible. Reporter Jonathan Webb guides you through an event which features the fastest fishermen in the business.

1.15 ITN NEWS

1.20 THE ITV SEVEN
John Oaksey at Doncaster introduces four races on this final day of the 1980 flat racing season, and Ken Butler at Windsor introduces three races 'over the sticks'. Your card:

1.30 Doncaster – Poppy H'cap (*5f.*)
1.45 Windsor – Buckinghamshire H'cap Chase (*2m.40yd*)
2.00 Doncaster – Steel Plate Autumn Stakes (*7f.*)
2.15 Windsor – Launderette Fortnight Stakes (H'cap Hurdle) (*2m.30yd*)
2.30 Doncaster – Amoco Jockeys Trophy (*7f.*)
2.45 Windsor – World-Wide Assurance Novices' Chase (*2m.40yd.*)
3.00 Doncaster – William Hill November H'cap (*1½m.*)

3.10 INTERNATIONAL SPORTS SPECIAL – 2
Karting
The Mazda Cars Race of Champions
from Hoddesdon, Herts.
Top home and overseas drivers contest the biggest and richest karting event ever staged in this country. It's a sport that breeds Grand Prix stars – such as the current world champion, Alan Jones. Today's main race of 25 laps is for karts of 100c.c. Without gears or clutch, they still top speeds of 75mph. In action, too, are the juniors – British schoolboys, between the ages of 13 and 16.

3.50 HALF-TIME SOCCER ROUND-UP

4.00 WRESTLING
from Lincoln

HEAVYWEIGHT: Big Pat Roach (Birmingham) v. Iron Duke
(Salford)
TAG MATCH: Big Daddy and Sammy Lee v. King Kong Kirk
and Sharky Ward
CATCHWEIGHT: Mick McMichael (Doncaster) v. The
American Dream (Miami, Florida)

4.50 RESULTS SERVICE

---

* Times are subject to change.

The show was hosted from 1968, till its demise in 1985, by the
Mallen-streaked Dickie Davies, Eamonn Andrews having chaired
proceedings when WoS started in 1965. Fred 'Gambit' Dineage and
ITV's answer to Steve Ryder, Jim Rosenthal, would step in as cover
when Dickie was off getting his hair done.

One of the iconic images of *World of Sport* was the array of
typists sitting behind the presenter. Viewers, including me, assumed
that these were reporters and secretaries busy collating all the latest
news and results from around the world. In fact, it was all for show,
they were actually admin staff for London Weekend Television
working on internal memos, letters, and the like.

Perhaps the two most famous segments of the show were *On the
Ball* and the wrestling.

On the Ball starred former footballers Ian St John and Jimmy
Greaves, who would banter their way through a 30-minute show
previewing the day's football fixtures. The pairing was so popular

that when *World of Sport* ended, their slot continued as a separate programme under the name *Saint & Greavsie*.

The wrestling was something of an anachronism in a sports show. This staged piece of pantomime did have a huge live following around the UK, and millions of people used to tune in at 4pm to watch goodies like Dynamite Kid take on baddies such as Mark 'Rollerball' Rocco. The two biggest stars, quite literally, were the 26-stone Big Daddy (Cheers!) and his nemesis, the 48-stone Giant Haystacks (Boo! Hiss!). Despite its loyal audience, it struggled to survive when *World of Sport* was pulled and finally gave way to the more flamboyant *WWF* from the US.

In 1985, ITV decided to stop broadcasting the programme. They were changing the way sport was to be shown on the channel, and an entire Saturday afternoon was seen as surplus to requirements. You could argue that they have never quite managed to attain the same level of success for their sports coverage since – their on-off relationship with Premier League highlights has become something of a running joke, never being able to compete with the BBC's *Match of the Day*, their brief flirtation with Formula 1 racing and the Oxford v. Cambridge boat race didn't really amount to much either, and now, with Sky dominating in almost every other area, they are left with Champions League football on weekday evenings for part of the year.

Dodo Rating: 🐥🐥🐥🐥🐥

Massive Viewing Figures

At various points during the '70s and '80s you could walk into the school playground or workplace in the morning, safe in the knowledge that everyone, everywhere, would have watched the same television programme the night before.

It is an experience that is unlikely to happen again. Unless the Queen dies or England ever make it to a World Cup Final.

Cast your mind back to the days of only four television channels. Heck, let's go back even further to the time when we only had BBC1, BBC2, and ITV. That was it. If you wanted to watch something on the telly, you had three choices.

As a result, the viewing audience would, from time to time, congregate around one televisual event: one live show, one soap episode, one sporting occasion, one sitcom. And because so many people were tuning in to the same thing, there was a shared sense of experience. When you laughed at Morecambe and Wise preparing breakfast in time to 'The Stripper', the whole nation was laughing with you. If you gasped at the sheer audacity of Den handing Angie the divorce papers on Christmas Day, the chances are that the rest of the people in your street were doing the same thing.

Let's look at some numbers, but not the usual ones you always hear about. When you study the most watched broadcasts in British television history, there are some remarkable examples.

- In November 1979, 23.95 million people watched the series finale of *To the Manor Born*.
- 22.22 million viewers tuned in to see an episode of *This is Your Life*. The subject? Lord Mountbatten. This was in 1977, Silver Jubilee year, so perhaps people were feeling particularly royalist.

- To put those two in perspective, a 'mere' 21.6 million turned on *Dallas* to find out who shot J.R.
- We know that Brits watched the wedding of Charles and Diana in their droves (28.4 million, to be precise), but that number was only slightly higher than the audience for the marriage of Princess Anne to Captain Mark Phillips (27.6 million) in 1973.
- Comedian Mike Yarwood is hardly held in the same sort of esteem as his contemporaries, such as Morecambe and Wise or The Two Ronnies, and yet his Christmas show in 1977 drew in 21.4 million, more than the others ever achieved.
- There are other oddities. The FA Cup Final replay between Chelsea and Leeds in 1970 was watched by more people (28.49 million) than any other sporting event in history, apart from England's World Cup Final victory in 1966 (32.3 million).
- And back in the days before dedicated film channels, a big premiere on terrestrial could really pull in the punters. The first showing of *Live and Let Die* on ITV in 1980 saw 23.5 million people tuning it. That's more than watched the infamous *Panorama* interview with Princess Diana in 1995.

These are remarkable numbers when you bear in mind that the most watched television show on Christmas Day 2010 was *Eastenders*, with 15.8 million viewers.

Dodo Rating: 🐔🐔🐔🐔

Closedown

Twenty-four-hour television is actually quite a new phenomenon, certainly in the UK. As recently at 1997, the BBC would effectively shut down every night at about 1am, not to resurface until breakfast television started in the morning. Instead of programmes, viewers would be treated to a test card or pages from Ceefax (both accompanied by some generic muzak), although there was a time when the transmitters were completely switched off, and all you could see was static.

But the BBC being the BBC, there was a certain regimen to be followed.

BBC1 would usually run through the next day's programmes, chuck in a quick weather report, and then play the national anthem while a clock ticked over on screen. BBC2 would sign off with the dulcet tones of the continuity announcer but, for some reason, no anthem.

With both channels, you would often get a few minutes of blank screen and then a voice would remind you: 'Don't forget to switch off your television set', which, if you had nodded off in the meantime, was enough to scare the living bejesus out of you.

Various ITV networks experimented with 24-hour television, but all channels had a closedown of sorts until the mid-1980s, and it wasn't until the introduction of satellite and cable to most homes that true 24-hour television really kicked in.

And while I, like many men, am quite happy to flick through 100 channels at two in the morning on the off-chance of a sex scene or car crash, and welcome the fact that I am able to do so, I do rather miss the polite good night that television used to offer viewers who had bothered to stay up until the early hours. I swear blind that I once heard a voice on BBC2 say something along the lines of:

'And from all of us here at BBC2, a very good night.'

[Long pause]

'Not that anyone is still up at this time. I am basically speaking to myself. I could pretty much say anything I wanted to. But I'd best not.'

[Another pause]

'Sweet dreams.'

At the time of writing, I note with interest that the BBC is considering bringing back closedown in a move to save money. So, perhaps this is one dodo that is about to be resurrected, although I wonder what will actually be shown on screen during the break in programming – a test card, pages from Ceefax? Could this spark a revival of many of the items listed in this section?

Probably not.

Dodo Rating: 🐦🐦🐦🐦🐦

Advertising Slogans

Some of the dodos featured in this book are not physical objects. They are not tangible things. They are ideas, concepts, or, in this case, phrases.

Some of the most famous advertising slogans and jingles of all time are ones that haven't actually been used for years – decades, even. Often the product they were thought up to sell doesn't even exist any more.

And yet they linger in the mind.

Why?

Well, I would argue that, like the very best song lyrics or beautiful lines of poetry, they have the ability to lodge in your brain and stay there forever.

Consider the following examples. How many can you remember?

A finger of Fudge is just enough to give your kids a treat.
If you like a lotta chocolate on your biscuit, join our club.
A man's gotta chew what a man's gotta chew.
Splash it all over.
You'll never put a better bit of butter on your knife.
For mash get Smash.
Do the Shake 'n' Vac and put the freshness back.
It's too orangey for crows.
Um Bongo, Um Bongo, they drink it in the Congo.
It's frothy man.
Tell them about the honey, mummy.
So big you gotta grin to get it in.
Everyone's a fruit and nut case.
I'm a secret lemonade drinker.
Birdseye Potato Waffles are waffly versatile.

Hands that do dishes can feel soft as your face, with mild green
    Fairy Liquid.

Rerecord, not fade away.

Happiness is a cigar called Hamlet.

What has a hazelnut in every bite?

Made to make your mouth water.

The Man from Del Monte, he say 'Yes!'

All because the lady loves Milk Tray.

Only the crumbliest, flakiest chocolate.

Two all beef patties, special sauce, lettuce, cheese, pickles,
    onions all wrapped up in a sesame seed bun.

Hello Tosh, Gotta Toshiba?

Anytime, anyplace, anywhere. There's a wonderful world you
    can share. It's the bright one, it's the right one, it's Martini.

Clunk Click every trip.

Refreshes the parts other beers cannot reach.

I bet he drinks Carling Black Label.

Nuts, whole hazelnuts, Cadburys take 'em and they cover them
    with chocolate.

Although they are no longer heard on the airwaves, lots of them
will live on for many years to come. They are like echoes of a time
gone by.

Dodo Rating: 🐔🐔🐔🐔

B-sides

In the golden age of the single, you were, of course, getting two songs, not one, every time you purchased a 7" from your local record shop – an A-side and a B-side.

Some artists used the B-side to get rid of any old material they had lying around the recording studio, or to lazily plonk another track from the album, but for many it was an opportunity to have some fun or to do something a bit different. For others, it ended up being where they put some of their finest songs.

Gene Vincent's very first single was a little ditty called 'Woman Love'. You could be forgiven for not knowing that, as it was deemed too risqué for radio play so DJs instead played the B-side, a song called 'Be-Bop-A-Lula'. The rest is rock and roll history.

'Gloria' by Them, 'Rain' by The Beatles, 'Erotic City' by Prince, 'Unchained Melody' by The Righteous Brothers, 'How Soon Is Now' by The Smiths, 'Maggie May' by Rod Stewart, even 'I Will Survive' by Gloria Gaynor, for goodness sake, all started out as B-sides.

The sleeves of singles often didn't list tracks as A-side or B-side, instead leading with the main track and tagging the support song as b/w or c/w (backed with and comes with). The A or B would appear on the label of the record itself.

The vast majority of B-sides would grace the flipside of a 7" single, never to appear anywhere else ever again, but some canny record executives realised the money-making potential of these rare tracks and many big acts have released B-side and rarity compilations over the years as a result.

One of the perverse things about the B-side, of course, was that many of them never got played at all. You had to physically flip the single over to play it on your turntable, and if you were obsessed with playing Olivia Newton John's 'Physical' over and over again while bouncing around in a leotard, you may never have got round to listening to 'The Promise (The Dolphin Song)'.

When consumers moved to favour the CD single during the '90s, the B-side still hung around, in theory, but with no need to turn over the disc, it just became an extra track or track two, and a lot of the mystique and magic was gone. Of course, with many bands still insisting on issuing vinyl singles, the B-side is still technically around, but no longer holds an important place in the musical firmament.

Dodo Rating: 🐦🐦🐦🐦🐦

Interludes

In the early days of television, much of the programming was live, so the schedule was not always as accurate as today. The BBC would often find itself with a bit of time to fill, and fill it they did, with a range of interludes – short films to keep viewers entertained until the next scheduled programme was ready to air.

The most famous of these is probably *The Potter's Wheel*, a five-and-a-half-minute black and while film of a potter (who only had his arms in shot) throwing a pot on a wheel. A quick YouTube search will find the clip today, and very soothing it is, too, accompanied as it is by 'The Young Ballerina' composed by Charles Williams, and played by the Queen's Hall Light Orchestra.

Other interludes included a spinning wheel, a windmill (the BBC clearly liked things that went round and round) and, by the magic of trick photography, the London to Brighton train run in four minutes. There was also a tropical beach, complete with crashing waves and pleasant breeze, and footage of a kitten playing with some wool and a wastebasket.

My personal favourites were the drawings and paintings done from scratch. You would see a blank sheet of paper and the artist's hands, and as the five minutes elapsed an owl or lion would be created in front of your eyes.

Dodo Rating:

Green Cross Code Man

Ask anyone born in the 1960s or 1970s to recite the Green Cross Code and they will almost certainly reply with:

STOP! LOOK! and LISTEN!

During the days of public information films, road safety was a message that was constantly being sent out, whether it was by Tufty the squirrel, Alvin Stardust, or Kevin Keegan. But by far the most memorable individual was the green and white superhero, the Green Cross Code Man.

Across a series of TV commercials he would materialise out of thin air whenever some long-haired urchin tried to cross a stereo-typical British street, often into the path of an oncoming Austin Allegro. Saving said oik from certain death, he would remind him of the safe way to cross, using the maxim:

'Always use the Green Cross Code, because I won't be there when you cross the road.'

Originally, I am led to believe, he would just say 'Always use the Green Cross Code', but that resulted in scores of children (idiots, clearly) running out into roads in the fervent expectation that the Green Cross Code Man would leap out to save them. At least, that's what the ones who survived claimed. As a result of which they added the second part of the sentence, which conveniently rhymed.

The films ran from the mid-'70s to 1990, and the Green Cross Code Man was played in each of them by Darth Vader himself, Dave Prowse. Dave, as many of you will know, is from the West Country and has quite a strong regional accent. He was famously dubbed by James Earl Jones in the *Star Wars* films. Sad to say, he was also dubbed in many of the Green Cross Code clips as well, but that didn't stop him from undoubtedly saving the lives of thousands of kids.

Now that's a real superhero!

Dodo Rating: 🐤🐤🐤🐤🐤

Television Stations

When I started researching this entry for the book, I was originally thinking about the regional independent stations of the '70s, '80s and '90s that didn't quite make it to the 21st century, stations such as Thames Television and TVS. But then I realised that we have lost dozens upon dozens of cable and satellite stations since the dawn of such technology.

Regional ITV franchises were weird things. Every ten years or so, ITV would renew its franchises by getting the existing holders to bid to keep their broadcast licence, while allowing other companies to bid as well. The deal was simple, the company that offered the most money, assuming they passed certain criteria, would get the franchise. These were sealed bids, so no one knew what the other companies were bidding.

Sounds fair enough, but it did lead to some anomalies. For example, no one ever tried to bid against Granada Television, presumably because they made *Coronation Street*, the nation's favourite soap opera at the time, and held the country to ransom over it. Or something like that. Basically, they didn't pay as much as other stations, and didn't have to worry about being outbid.

Other regions, such as London and the South East, were hotbeds of competition, and this meant that from time to time the TV channel you were used to watching vanished completely. I remember when Thames changed to Carlton but you may have lived in a region covered by TVS, Tyne Tees, or HTV; each of which is no more.

It may seem like a small thing but when your childhood of TV watching is punctuated by the same TV ident every day – such as Thames Television's London skyline emerging from the River Thames – then their passing is worthy of note.

But like I said, there have been loads more casualties in recent years. Do you remember any of these?

Auction World TV, Bravo, Carlton Food Network, Comedy Channel, ITV News, L!ve TV, Lifestyle, Men & Motors, Open Access, Teachers TV, UK Horizons.

And what about Landscape? It was around in the early days of satellite television. New age music played along to moody videos of birds in flight or paradise beaches.

There are plenty more, but time to move on.

Dodo Rating: 🐦🐦🐦🐦🐦

The Watershed

Yes, I know it still technically exists and, don't worry, I am not about to come over all Mary Whitehouse on you, but I am sure many of you remember the days when the watershed actually used to mean something.

No swearing, no tits, no arses, no willies, and definitely no female private parts before 9pm. TV stations would also avoid any themes of a remotely adult nature and films would often be edited and censored to remove any 'questionable' content. There simply was nothing salacious to see before the watershed.

Clearly any really explicit content is still kept till after the watershed, but adult themes and storylines pervade most TV dramas that air in the early evening – just think about the plots of *Eastenders* or *Coronation Street*, for example. It also seems that, over time, some former after-9pm shows have come to be considered suitable for earlier viewing, especially on digital and satellite channels. *Blackadder* is fairly easy to find on one of the comedy stations at any time of the day, but was originally shown at 9pm on BBC2. *Friends* is rated 12 on DVD, but is often shown on Channel 4 in the early morning at the weekend. And there are many more examples.

Obviously our standards and morals change over the years – imagine *The Young Ones* being broadcast in the '50s or '60s! – and I am sure they will continue do so, but something of the frisson has been lost in the last decade or so. The excitement of discovering something forbidden – be it sex, violence, adult themes, or just some ribald comedy – has pretty much evaporated. And I am talking about teenagers here, young adults on a voyage of discovery. I don't even want to get into what younger kids have access to these days.

I shudder to think.

Dodo Rating: 🐤🐤🐤

Analogue Television

By the end of 2012, any remaining analogue television signals will be switched off in favour of digital. In order to roll out digital broadcasts, the powers that be need to free up space, and can only complete the project by getting rid of analogue altogether.

So gone once and for all are the days of twiddling with the portable aerial on front of the telly, Dad being forced to stand in the corner of the room with his arm aloft so that Mum can see the end of the film she is watching, and that fuzzy bit of snow on screen when a plane flies past.

So no great loss, then?

Well, probably not, for most people. Digital television delivers a better-quality picture, better sound, more channels, more choice, and, in many cases, lots of fancy extras.

But the digital signal will only reach 98.5% of the country; 1.5% of the population will, presumably, have no TV signal at all. That's almost 1 million people. What will they do? Where do they live? I presume they are at the top of mountains, in deep valleys, or remote islands, but nearly a million of the blighters? Blimey.

So progress may be great, but it is only of use if it can actually reach you.

I love the idea, stupid and fanciful though it is, of some residual analogue signal floating around that these people can pick up on their old TV sets. They would end up living in a time bubble of old episodes of *Porridge*, *Play School*, and *Terry & June*. Sounds quite nice to me. I'd be tempted to pay them a visit.

Dodo Rating: 🐤🐤🐤🐤

Teletext

When that final analogue signal is switched off, it will mark the death of Ceefax, the only remaining teletext service in the UK. Hopefully this won't happen halfway through a football match, with fans waiting for an update on the score as the screen refreshes, a popular pastime in the days before Sky Sports.

The BBC launched its teletext service, called Ceefax because it allowed you to 'see' the 'facts', in 1974. It was born out of technology used to create subtitles for the deaf, and started out with a few dozen pages of information that could be accessed by punching in a page number on your remote control.

ITV launched its own service, Oracle, in the same year, and each of the five terrestrial channels had their own service at one time or another. As teletext grew, it added a huge array of content and became an essential source of up-to-the-minute information for most households. Don't forget, this was before the days of the internet and 24-hour rolling news; if you wanted the most up to date information, teletext was the place to look.

It led, understandably, with news and sport (live football scores during match day being a particularly popular feature) but widened its brief to include more niche interests and magazine content. Channel 4 had excellent music review and news pages, there was an interactive quiz called *Bamboozle** in which you answered the questions by punching in numbers, and horse racing analysis and cards worked brilliantly on the format, with the BBC's Ceefax pundit being a particularly successful tipster.

There were gardening pages, knitting pages with full patterns, computer pages with programs to input, kids' pages, advent

---

* Update: *This has now been launched as an App.*

calendars at Christmas, and joke pages (you pressed the REVEAL button of the remote to show the punchlines).

But even if you never pressed the TEXT button on your remote control, you would get to see Ceefax, and listen to some muzak, when *Pages from Ceefax* was broadcast late at night or early in the morning. Used as a bit of a filler when there were no actual programmes to air, the viewer would be treated to a rolling loop of the most popular pages with an easy listening soundtrack. It may not sound particularly inspirational, but most of us would have spent a few minutes in front of it at some point in our lives, often while eating a bowl of cornflakes.

ITV stopped its teletext service in 2009, and Ceefax is only available nowadays via your analogue signal (although *Pages from Ceefax* is still occasionally broadcast on BBC2), which, as mentioned, is soon to vanish. It has been replaced with the flashy graphics and interactivity of modern digital systems, which do look to come from another century entirely (perhaps because they do) but somehow lack the warm, friendly feel of teletext of old. Thankfully, you can find examples of pretty much every page there ever was at one of several online resources; well worth a visit for all you nostalgia junkies.

Dodo Rating: 🐦🐦🐦🐦

AT THE CUTTING EDGE
OF TECHNOLOGY

Crushed beneath the wheels of progress ...

Audio Cassettes

No single entry epitomises the philosophy of this book more than the humble cassette tape. Its fascinating story captures everything that *21st Century Dodos* is all about – a new piece of technology rises to become a world leader, installs itself in popular culture, becomes part of everyday life for billions of people …

… but finds itself crushed beneath the wheels of progress, and is now an endangered species.

Despite this, it has left an indelible mark on generations, a legacy that is worth recording (sorry!) here for posterity.

Tape as a recording medium had been around for many years before the compact cassette made its debut in 1962, but it mainly consisted of cumbersome reel-to-reel tapes which were OK for the professionals, but never really took hold in the world of home entertainment.

So, when Dutch company Philips unveiled the compact version, it created a considerable stir. Essentially a reel-to-reel tape shrunk down in size and squeezed into a plastic casing, it was portable, durable, could be played on both sides, and, crucially, was re-recordable. But it wasn't until Philips agreed to license the format to other manufacturers for no fee that it truly took hold and revolutionised the industry.

In the early days, it was intended purely as a recording device, and cassette players of the era were set up for ease of recording with little emphasis on high-fidelity sound. They were used mainly for dictation, in office and professional work. Sound quality and repro-duction were not great, and certainly nowhere near as good as vinyl records, so early attempts to sell pre-recorded music cassettes were not a huge success.

But the companies behind the format kept on tweaking and improving it, and once chromium dioxide tape and Dolby sound reduction were introduced, the music cassette became a viable format to rack alongside LPs and 8-track cartridges in record shops.

The real catalyst to global domination, however, was the invention in the late 1970s of the Sony Walkman. This portable device, not much bigger than a cassette itself, allowed people to listen to music on the move. As a result, during the 1980s, the cassette overtook vinyl to become the most popular music format.

The other major reason for its success was the fact that you could record pretty much anything you wanted onto a blank cassette. Whether it be a mixtape for your girlfriend (more on which later), the best bits of the Top 40 chart show (where the skill was to start and stop recording at just the right point to avoid taping the DJ), a copy of your favourite disco album to listen to while out roller-skating (which appeared to be what everyone in America was doing), or just personal reflections, it was a way to preserve audio that had not been available in the home before. And it was this element that, in my opinion, changed the world.

Take the punk movement, for example. The whole DIY music philosophy was able to thrive because bands could record songs in their garage, duplicate them, knock up dodgy photocopied covers, and distribute to friends, journalists, and, inevitably, John Peel. Peel's legendary radio show broadcast the debuts of countless bands, the vast majority of which sank without trace, but a select few went on to create music that influenced the generations that followed. And all of these bands, at least during the '70s and '80s, got their first play on his show by sending in a demo tape.

Former Communist countries were able to listen to Western music via tapes recorded from the radio or smuggled in from outside (their small size much easier to hide than 12" records). Outlawed political and religious movements used cassettes to spread the word. Audiobooks, already a popular format in their own right, became more freely available, and finally brought the joy of books to many blind children and adults who could not read or get access to Braille editions. Cassette tapes were also the original format for software on early home computers (I'll bang on about that in a little while).

The in-car cassette player only increased their popularity. Most cars had had radios installed as standard for some time, a few came with 8-track cartridge players, but the tape deck brought pre-recorded music to the daily commute or boring motorway journey (cue opening bars of 'Born to be Wild' or 'The Chain').

They really were everywhere. Huge dumpbins (as they were known in the trade) of blank tapes were on sale in every record shop and electrical store. You could buy many different types, both in terms of recording quality (to be honest, I never really understood the difference, and was never convinced to shell out for a posh 'metal' tape – it would have been a bit pointless when all I was doing was taping from the radio and creating mixtapes) and recording length. The most popular formats were C60 (30 minutes each side), C90 (45 minutes each side), and C120 (oh, you get the idea), but there was a myriad of other versions ranging from C15 (for answer phones and Dictaphones) to C240 (which were crap and kept getting chewed up).

You could use them time and time again, and even the pre-recorded ones could be taped over. We have all at one point or another nicked mum's Acker Bilk *Best Of*, stuck a bit of Sellotape over the corner (or 'write-protect tab', to give it its proper name), just in time to record the best bits of the Top 40.

Despite its success, the format was not without its problems, the most troubling of which, for the music industry at least, was the explosion of piracy. Suddenly, any Tom, Dick, or Harry could make a cheap recording of a an LP and sell it, or pass it on for free. And piracy did indeed become a big problem, with huge networks of crooks reproducing bestselling albums on tape in bulk, and selling them at market stalls, in pubs, and out of the back of lorries. Many did attempt to make the finished item look legit, but the majority of pirated tapes coming out of the Far East were, shall we say, well dodgy.

While the millionaire record executives did attempt to clamp down on this illegal black market, they also tried to scare the people at home with their staggeringly unsuccessful 'Home Taping is Killing Music' campaign, featuring a cassette skull and crossbones. Their point, and they did have one, was that every time you taped a copy of the new Madness album to give to your mate, that was a few quid that didn't find its way into their bulging pockets or get to the rather more deserving artists themselves.

What the campaign failed to recognise was that the mixtape culture, the idea of creating your own compilation and sharing it with friends, was as powerful a source of recommendation, new music and discovery as any radio station, TV show, or advertising campaign. It is pretty much accepted now that for every pound lost to a pirate tape, at least the same came into the industry from someone who had just discovered Blondie via a compilation made by Dave in Year 5.

There were physical problems with the format as well. Not every cassette player was calibrated to play at the same speed, so you could sometimes find yourself listening to Barry White but it sounding more like the Bee Gees. Their compact size meant they were a lot easier to lose than their 12" vinyl counterpart. They were also completely buggered if you stepped on them.

The most common issue was that they would quite frequently get chewed up. A worrying warble in the vocals would warn you that it was coming, and then the music could come to a complete stop. You'd open up the cassette deck to discover anything from a few inches to several feet of dark brown tape being spewed out. If you were lucky and the whole thing wasn't mangled beyond salvation, you could remedy matters by inserting a pencil into one of the reels and manually rewinding it by hand, either by patiently twisting or, my preferred method, by spinning it around like a football rattle.

The advent of the compact disc spelled the demise of the compact cassette. Although they valiantly held their own for most of the 1990s, helped by the sheer proliferation of players, car stereos and the fact that lots of people hadn't got round to buying CD players yet, most record companies had ceased production by the beginning of the new millennium due to lack of demand.

Sales of blank tapes limped on. By 1988, over 3 billion blank cassettes had been sold in the UK, at a peak of 50 million a year. By 2007, this had slipped to 5 million, and numbers were plummeting fast.

However, there might be some light at the end of the tunnel. TDK, one of the leading manufacturers of blank tapes, reports sales slowly beginning to rise. No one is quite sure why, but theories include the fact that people are still buying them for cars or at home, the police still have to use tape for any suspect interviews and, in a bizarre twist, new bands are often distributing their music by cassette as the format is now so difficult to pirate in our digital age.

So, while the heyday of the cassette is definitely behind us, it seems that a small number may survive for a while yet.

Dodo Rating:

Mixtapes

Creating the perfect mixtape took hours of planning.

First, you'd have to decide what sort of theme you were going for. Just a collection of favourite songs to play in the car was fine, but there were many more speciality areas, of which these are just a few:

Potential New Girlfriend/Boyfriend Mix. Possibly the most important of all mixtapes, a group of songs intended, often through subliminal messages, to persuade a potential partner what a splendid catch you were – witty, well-rounded, thoughtful, and with great taste in music. Song choice would almost always be a blend of your all-time faves (if they don't like 'This Must Be the Place', then they clearly aren't the one for me) and songs that sort of hinted at the fact that you wanted to get into their pants. You needed to be subtle, but not too subtle. The recipient was to be left in little doubt that you were up for it, but the content would be ambiguous enough that you could deny all if they proved to be less than keen. Countless romances were started in this way. Millions of children walk the earth today because dad chose to place 'Friday I'm in Love' by The Cure next to 'The You and Me Song' by The Wannadies. Or something like that.

Party Tape. For lazy DJs everywhere. A couple of well-sequenced C90s could ensure even the dullest party had a bit of a buzz about it, and leave the host plenty of time to wander round with canapés instead of mixin' and scratchin' at the turntables. This mix would be filled with plenty of uptempo tracks to dance to, a handful of singalong classics, and the obligatory run of three slow songs, timed to come on towards the end of the evening when there was plenty of snogging to be done.

Impress Your Friends. The teenage muso, and those quite a bit older, to be fair, would often share mixes with fellow music-enthusiast schoolmates and friends. These were crucial in securing your position in the social hierarchy, and balance was the key. You needed just enough recognisable-but-not-too-obvious stuff (lesser-known album tracks from popular new-wave bands were ideal) plus some indie anthems ('God, I love that song, man. Good choice'), topped off with a sprinkling of really obscure songs that no one else would have heard. Even the geekiest nerd could shoot up the popularity charts if word got out that he had some REM demo tracks and that Violent Femmes' song with the swearing on his last mixtape.

Linked Themes. Mixtapes could take on any theme: Christmas songs, cover versions, driving, tracks to work out to; the list is endless. I was once given a mix where each song title contained a word from the song title before. It was shit.

The Break-up Tape. Sadly, not every tape sent to a potential partner led to love, marriage, and happily-ever-after. The majority of relationships came a cropper, and that would inevitably result in a break-up tape, and no more sorry an example of wallowing in self-pity has ever been witnessed in popular culture. Whether it included 'All By Myself' by Eric Carmen, 'I Want You' by Elvis Costello (surely the most heartbreaking song ever?) or 'Without You' by Harry Nilsson, they were painful to listen to, on an emotional level at least. Thankfully, most break-up tapes never got sent to the ex and were just played repeatedly in darkened bedrooms to the backdrop of self-indulgent sobs.

Nowadays, of course, mixtapes have been largely replaced by Spotify playlists, iTunes mixes and the habit of burning CDs, but though these represent technological progress, they lack the heart, the soul and the sheer effort of their cassette-based predecessor.

And that is where a mixtape wins every time. If I were to create one for you, I would spend hours, days even, going through my records and CDs to compile the perfect tracklisting, a collection of songs that was just the right balance between stuff I like and stuff I think you would like. This would almost certainly be written down in a spiral-bound notebook, and go through many revisions before it was ready to be recorded.

Running order and sequencing were everything. Some songs naturally work well when placed together on a mixtape; others jar or clash. Tempo changes need to be handled with skill – moving from a piece of thrash metal to some ambient dance might work, but it requires planning, a brave attitude, and a rather diverse record collection.

Once all that was sorted, the physicality of the process would kick in, if that's not too pompous an expression (I know it is, but it's my book so I am using it anyway). I would have to arrange all the albums so they were in the right order for recording, taking each one in turn, queuing up the correct track on the turntable or CD player before dropping the stylus or pressing play, and then immediately releasing the PAUSE button on the tape deck. Any slip of the hand or delay and I'd miss the start of the track and have to rewind and start again.

It was something that took a lot of time. The fact that I would spend hours working on a mixtape spoke volumes about my opinion of the recipient. Consequently, a mixtape beats a CD or playlist. It just does.

And I haven't even mentioned the artwork. Blank tapes came with a liner card, usually on the reverse side of the packaging, with space for you to write the tracklisting. Well, I say space, but there was never enough of it. A small grid might allow you to jot down

'Stop' by Sam Brown, but was no use whatsoever if your mixtape included 'It's The End of the World as We Know It (And I Feel Fine)' by REM. Consequently, many mixtape compilers customised their covers by either ignoring the lines completely and creating elaborate spidery biro listings or, preferably, by creating their own covers by hand.

Entire books and exhibitions have been dedicated to mixtape art, most notably *Mix Tape: The Art of Cassette Culture* by Thurston Moore of the band Sonic Youth (who claims to only listen to music on cassette, although I think he might be fibbing). It was a whole subgenre of creativity, adding even further to the personal nature of the object itself. I once received a pop-up tracklisting from a girlfriend, and though she later dumped me for some tosser in the year above, she retains a small corner of my heart for the effort she put into the mixtape alone.

Dodo Rating: 🐦🐦🐦🐦

VHS

Ahh, who's gloating now, eh, VHS? You thought you had won the war when you saw off the technically superior, but undoubtedly less popular, Betamax, didn't you? There you were as the King of Home Entertainment, happily lording it up over laserdiscs and anything else that came along, only for you to be made almost completely irrelevant by the onset of digital technology.

To add insult to injury when I tried to donate some videotapes to my local charity shop recently, they refused to take them. 'No one wants these any more, love,' said the delightful old lady in the polyester dress.

Oh, VHS, how did it come to this?

The Video Home System (or VHS, for short) burst into our living rooms in the late 1970s. It had been created by JVC in Japan, who realised that the road to world domination lay in sharing the technology, so they licensed it to other manufacturers to ensure a wide range of machines were on the market.

The very first video cassette recorders (VCRs) went on sale in 1977, but were, to begin with, very much a luxury item. Once prices started to come down they became far more popular, and by the time the '80s were in full flow they were a common feature in many homes below, or above, the TV set.

Video had two major attractions. One was the fact that you could now watch films on your television when you wanted to, not just when the three (count them!) TV stations chose to broadcast them. The other was the ability to record programmes to watch later.

The film thing was really a very big deal at the time, something we can often forget in this age of Sky Movies, LoveFilm, and internet streaming. For one thing, the UK didn't get to see US films in the cinema until quite a while, often months, after America, something I talk about in more detail in a later entry. Outside of the cinema, the only place to watch a film was on the telly, but TV stations did not get to show the big Hollywood blockbusters until years after release. Because of this, the first showing of a big film on BBC1 or ITV was a major deal, and there would be trailers for weeks beforehand, often resulting in huge viewing figures. For example, *Jaws* premiered on UK television on ITV on 8 October 1981. It had first been shown in cinemas in 1975, six years earlier! That night, 23.25 million people tuned in to watch it, just under half of the entire population, and more than the peak audience for the Royal Wedding between William and Kate in 2011.

So you can see why the home video rental market exploded as the '80s went on. Every town, and almost every village, had its own rental store, and people had access to thousands of films whenever they wanted to see them, changing the sorts of films we watched. This was before the day of the multiplex cinema, and most local film theatres only had two screens. Two cinema screens and three TV channels did not really offer a huge selection, but all of a sudden we had video stores with aisles of cassettes. This meant that you could rent a new film, or perhaps an old classic, but you could also borrow all sorts of shite you had never heard of – the straight-to-video market was born.

The appetite for watching films at home was so great that it was difficult to meet the demand. Studios realised that consumers would potentially watch almost anything, especially if all the block-busters were out of stock at 8pm on a Saturday night, and films that had previously sat on distributors' shelves unwatched and unloved were quickly converted to VHS and sent out. All manner of low-budget thrillers, action films, or true-life stories (most of which seemed to feature Brian Dennehy) found audiences that simply hadn't been there before.

And then there was the porn. At one end of the scale, the legal end, a plethora of erotic films hit the market. They were incredibly tame compared to the explicit material that is only a Google search away for people today, but they were pretty much all that the average person (OK, let's face it, bloke) could get access to at the time. Every video store had a top shelf full of the stuff. At the other end was the hardcore pornography that was illegal in the UK, but was exploding across the US. Much of it found its way here. It is said that the porn industry is often the first to exploit new technology, and that can certainly be argued when it came to VHS.

Such material was not without its understandable controversy, but it wasn't so much the pornography that was dismaying the *Daily Mail* readers of the '80s. They really had it in for horror films, the so-called 'video nasties'. Titles such as *The Texas Chainsaw Massacre* and *Evil Dead* were banned in the UK for many years, despite them now being seen as classics of the genre and the inspiration for many of the major directors of today.

Home recording was the other big feature of the VCR. Never before had you been able to watch a TV programme if you weren't sitting down in front of your set as it was broadcast. Early machines were famously hard to programme and this led to numerous devices languishing in living rooms flashing 00:00 for weeks on end, but, once mastered, users were able to record what they wanted, when they wanted. Never again did you have to miss an episode of *Neighbours* (especially that one where Bronwyn did a bellydance, or the one where Henry wound up naked in Mrs Mangle's garden), or the show jumping on *Grandstand*.

Most homes built up a significant library of recordings, piles of blank tapes lying around, each with handwritten scribbles on the stickers. There were endless family arguments over 'Which idiot taped over *Dallas*?!' You could buy fancy plastic cases, often modelled to look like hardback books, so as to house your collection with more style. The VHS was a fundamental part of the social fabric throughout the '80s.

The early '90s saw another big leap in VHS use, with a growing market for purchasing, as opposed to renting, films on video. For a long time the cost of films on video had been kept high – typically between £30 and £75 so as to encourage people to rent them rather than purchase. Hardly anyone was going to pay £50 for a copy of *The Toxic Avenger* so your local video store coughed up on your behalf and then hoped to rent it out for more than 50 times at £1 a go, or something like that. As the '80s came to an end, film companies realised that there was a significant desire for people to own their favourite films or TV shows, and most big films started to be issued in cheaper editions, six months to a year after the rental copy.

When you consider the speed with which technology is developing these days, it is testament to the durability and success of VHS that it has only really died out as we have entered the 21st century.

The better quality and extra bonus materials available through DVD won people over at the end of the '90s and saw many replacing their VHS collections with this more expensive, but far sexier, new format. The launch of Sky+ and other personal video recorders changed the way we recorded TV content. As the 2000s came to a close, the manufacture of pre-recorded video cassettes had pretty much ceased, with only a handful of films being released in the format, and this was often more of a marketing exercise, such as with the film *Paranormal Activity*, than anything else.

Many people still own a VCR for watching home films or all the old stuff they have on tape, but the transition to digital is fast apace and the sturdy oblong video cassette is soon to be no more.

Dodo Rating:

Betamax

Despite the fact that Betamax came out two years before VHS, and was widely perceived to be of better quality, it ultimately lost the battle with its younger, chunkier partner, and became a classic example of how not to establish a new technology format in the marketplace.

Sony created Betamax for the professional and home user in 1975, but made a few bad judgement calls which meant that they went from 100% of the market upon launch, to 7.5% only ten years later.

JVC tried to make VHS as cheap and widely available as possible, licensing the technology to many other companies. Sony attempted to hold on to the perception of quality, thereby ending up with fewer machines on the market at a higher price. Consumers were eager to own video players, but were not keen to spend thousands of pounds on them, with many opting to rent. In the UK, the leading rental shops were part-owned by JVC so they really got behind VHS, and it wasn't long before the format dominated. So much so that anyone owning a Betamax felt like a bit of a numpty, and no amount of declaring, 'But the picture quality is amazing' really made them feel any better.

Betamax wasn't helped by the fact that it had a shorter running time than VHS, especially in the US with the NTSC format. Sony also made the decision not to allow porn on Betamax. Many analysts believe this last point to be the biggest reason for its failure – a sure sign of our times.

By the late '80s, Sony pretty much knew the game was up, and started getting into the VHS market themselves. The last Betamax machine was produced in 2002.

But at least Sony learnt from their mistakes and were never again to see a new format fail in this way. Just look at the huge global dominance of the minidisc!

Dodo Rating: 🐦🐦🐦🐦🐦

Minidiscs

Such is the fast moving nature of technology that some inventions seem to die out within a short time of being born. This was the case with the minidisc.

Sony launched it in 1992 as the future of home recording, and it was intended as a high-quality alternative to analogue cassettes. With music lovers converting their album collections to compact disc, it made sense that they would want similar quality for the stuff they recorded at home, didn't it?

The minidisc hit problems early on because it found itself up against the digital compact cassette (DCC) from Philips, and consumers weren't sure which format to go for. Sony put their weight behind their invention by releasing albums by lots of Sony artists on the format, and also by licensing the technology to other hardware manufacturers, thereby increasing the number of players on the market.

Ultimately, though, people just weren't all that fussed about digital home recording. They were perfectly happy paying a few quid for a five-pack of TDK blank tapes, as they were mainly using them for mixtapes, voice recordings, and other stuff that didn't rely on incredible sound quality. The format was popular with professionals, and some studios still use them to this day, but the high price just put most punters off.

Anyway, less than a decade after the minidisc, a small white oblong called an iPod was launched, pretty much changing the face of portable music forever.

Dodo Rating: 🐤🐤🐤🐤

Laserdiscs

They were the future, they really were.

But now the future has arrived they are nowhere to be seen.

Laserdiscs hit the market in the late '70s, offering a high-quality alternative to VHS and Betamax video cassettes. A forerunner to both the CD and DVD, they were much larger than those formats – just a little bit smaller than a 12" record – were double-sided, and contained analogue data, rather than digital.

Picture quality was better than video, but discs and players were a lot more expensive so, in the UK at least, sales were restricted to early adopters and show-offs with loads of cash to piss away on fancy gadgets. There was a better take up in the US, and the format was a success in the Far East, particularly in Japan.

As the technology improved, the discs were able to carry and process digital image data as well as additional audio tracks. The first director's commentary was on a laserdisc, an idea that DVDs made their own nearly 20 years later.

Ultimately, they just didn't catch on over here. VHS tapes dominated the market and there simply wasn't the range of titles available, or the enthusiasm from retailers, to give laserdiscs the kickstart they needed. It didn't help that longer films had to be spread over two or more discs, and in the end they were consigned to the cupboard marked 'Nice Idea, Wrong Time'.

Dodo Rating:

Polaroid Cameras

It is rare for us to come close to understanding what it was like for Neanderthal man to discover fire or for Victorians to witness electric light, how the first people to watch a cinema projection of a steam train ran out of the theatre in fear, or the sheer wonder of the first television pictures.

But anyone who was around when Polaroid cameras came out will have some inkling.

That first shot, the picture being ejected with a robotic whir, ripping the protective wrapper off and then watching as slowly, ever so slowly, an image began to emerge.

It was magic, sheer magic. The stuff of witches, wizards, and sorcery.

Instant cameras (they weren't just made by Polaroid but their name became synonymous with the technology, just as Hoover's did with vacuum cleaners) had been around since the '60s, but it was in the '70s that they started turning up in people's homes and were more widely used. The distinctive print with its thick white border has become an icon.

In this modern age of digital cameras, the Polaroid is viewed as an antique, although it still has a cult following. The company announced that it was ceasing production of instant film in 2008, but had to reverse the decision a year later due to overwhelming public demand.

So, not quite extinct yet, but certainly endangered.

Dodo Rating: 🐤🐤🐤

Home Computers

By which I mean that legendary array of plastic boxes that invaded our homes during the 1980s and seemed remarkably cool at the time, but actually had less memory power than it has taken my laptop to type this paragraph.

Today our homes are full of notebooks (the computer version!), iPads, desktop PCs, Playstations, Wiis, Xboxes, and hand-held consoles, and we spend our time playing photo-realistic war games, challenging people on the other side of the planet to games of Scrabble, and hurling angry birds at a group of military pigs.

Back then it was the ZX Spectrum, Vic 20, and BBC Micro, and we lost hours trying to guide a miner through a series of caves, taking a bloke called Horace skiing, and typing out 'PICK UP SWORD' and 'GO EAST' on text adventure games.

But here's the thing, we would never have had the former without the latter, no matter how quaint and antiquated they may seem today.

Here is a quick whistle-stop tour through some of the more iconic home computers of the time.

Sinclair ZX81

The first home computer that you could purchase from the high street, the ZX81, was the brainchild of calculator king Clive Sinclair, and, launched in 1981, sold over a million units. There were computers available for home use before, most notably its predecessor the ZX80, but they all came in kit form and had to be soldered together. The modern, sleek ZX81 came pre-assembled and pretty much ready to go.

Weighing in with a whopping 1KB of memory (check the size of the next email you send and compare), it had no moving parts and relied on a membrane keyboard (you just pressed hard on the plastic shell) and plugged straight into your television. You could expand the memory with a RAM pack that slotted into the back, cranking power up to 16KB (again, check that against the size of one email today) but the pack was top-heavy and often had to be stuck to the main computer with sticky tape. There was also a printer, a small device that appeared to use that shiny toilet roll they used to have at primary school.

Of course, the greatest achievement of all the 1980s home computers was that they brought gaming into the home and, even though they seem prehistoric by today's standards, ZX81 games such as *Flight Simulator* and *3-D Monster Maze* have now achieved legendary status.

Sinclair ZX Spectrum

The follow-up to the ZX81 came out a year later, and boasted colour graphics rather than the monochrome of its elder sibling. It was the home computer that truly revolutionised the industry, selling over 5 million units in its various guises, and launching some of the most popular computer games ever.

It was an odd beast, though, and not the most practical of machines. The rubber keys on the keyboard contained multi-functions that could only be accessed by pressing SHIFT or ALT or other more elaborate combinations, and I am pretty sure there are some functions that have still never been used to this day. The rubber keys also made it a bit of a pain to type on, so it lost out in the home programming stakes to its more robust competitors. However, most users only ever pressed Z to move left, X to move right, W to go up, and S to go down, anyway. Sinclair finally relented and included a more traditional keyboard on later models, but the rubber keys remain the distinctive feature of the Spectrum.

Although the early models came with no joystick ports, the Spectrum was a popular gaming machine and spawned numerous classics such as *Manic Miner*, *Jet Set Willy*, *Horace Goes Skiing*, *The Hobbit*, *Daley Thompson's Decathlon*, and *Lords of Midnight*. It is credited with inspiring a generation of gamers who went on to create the classics of the 1990s and 2000s.

Commodore Vic 20

Despite the fact that it had lower memory than its competitors (3.5KB compared to the Spectrum's 16KB), the Vic 20 became the first home computer to sell a million copies, and was one of the most successful machines in both the US and the UK.

Part of the appeal was just the look and feel of the thing. Unlike the Sinclair models, this actually had a proper keyboard, and was large and impressive. You could touch type on it, which made it easier for home programming, and it was a robust piece of kit.

It could never quite live up to the Spectrum's game play but it did its best to hold its own, and games such as *The Wizard and the Princess* and *Wacky Waiters* became classics of the format.

It only lasted a couple of years, though, as the Commodore 64 that followed was much more powerful, and had better graphics. Nonetheless, the Vic 20 was the first computer for many people still in the industry today and is much cherished by those who owned one back then.

Commodore 64

Bigger, more powerful, and in a darker shade of beige, the Commodore 64 became the bestselling home computer of all time, with nearly 17 million machines sold. A big hit in the US, where most of its owners were located, it did not perhaps have the cult gaming appeal in the UK that the Spectrum had, but it was a solid, dependable family computer, and the first such machine that many people owned.

BBC Micro

Education, education, education. Designed and manufactured by Acorn Computers, but supported by the BBC as part of their Computer Literacy Project, this was the machine to be found in schools. The BBC branding added a certain credibility to the machine, enabling Middle England to trust this new fangled device and allow it into their homes. When Computer Studies first hit the timetable, initially as an out-of-hours voluntary lesson, it was usually a BBC Micro that pupils learnt on, supported by a range of TV programming.

Never very cool, the BBC Micro was probably doomed by its association with the classroom. Kids wanted a Spectrum or Vic 20 to play on at home. It was also about twice the price of its more fun competitors, so never quite made it into sufficient homes to secure any traction. It remains, however, the machine that many people learnt to program on.

Dodo Rating: 🐥🐥🐥🐥

Loading Computer Games from Tape

Of course, the games for all of the home computers just mentioned were loaded up by playing a cassette tape. Any tape player would do, but those rectangular box machines were the most commonly used. You would connect one to your computer with a cable, type 'LOAD MANIC MINER', or whatever the game was called, and then press PLAY.

A series of peculiar beeps, whirs, clicks, and general fuzziness would then be heard as the tape player communicated with the computer. Sometimes, with a bit of luck, the tape would get to the end, and the program would have loaded successfully, but the strike rate wasn't great. It could take a few attempts to get it right.

There were no short cuts, either. A game could take five minutes or so to load, and you would invariably be looking at the screen waiting for something to happen. No Windows progress bars in those days. And you would have to go through the same process every single time you played the game. None of this download once and then it was on your computer for good. Oh no, if you wanted a quick game of *Horace Goes Skiing* after school, then you needed to twiddle your thumbs for a while first.

Progress is a wonderful thing. I can download an app to my phone within seconds and it will stay there forever, if I want. One click and I am checking a map, throwing an angry bird at a pig, or reading the latest news headlines. So why am I nostalgic for a time when it would take bloody ages, and usually two or three attempts, to get anything loaded?

I have no idea.

Dodo Rating: 🐦🐦🐦🐦🐦

Printer Paper with Holes

Next time your computer printer jams, runs out of ink, or fails to work wirelessly, cast your mind back to the early days of home computing and the very first computer printers.

Huge dot-matrix blighters, with the most impractical and bizarre paper. Long perforated rolls, rather like a giant's toilet roll, with holes punched at regular intervals running parallel along each side. You had to feed the holes onto some prongs and then hand-crank the thing along until it was in place, and then wait 20 minutes while a device a bit like *Grandstand*'s vidiprinter spewed out vaguely readable text.

Compare a printout from a Commodore 64 to the flashy colour stuff we get today. This is all in recent memory, people; we really have come this far.

If you ever had to deal with this stuff, you will never forget it. But I doubt that you miss it.

Dodo Rating: 🐦🐦🐦🐦🐦

Dial-up Modems

With the advent of broadband internet connections and wireless connectivity, one relatively recent technological development is rapidly becoming endangered.

Less than ten years ago, if you had a home internet connection, then it would almost certainly have been dial-up. By which I mean that your computer modem would use your telephone line to call up your internet provider and connect to the service.

This little box of mysterious flashing lights and wires would let you know it was doing its job by relaying the sounds of the phone call through your computer:

[dial tone]
[sound of a phone ringing]
blleeeep burgh krpphgspreeksplangkerlungkerlungkerlung
[pause]
bleepsping plonk plonkkerchang dank dank ding
[ad lib to fade]

By the end of which you would, six or seven times out of ten, be connected to the internet. But, boy, would it be slow. Dial-up internet connections were typically 56 kilobits per second, which is 12½ times slower than the slowest broadband connection. To put that in perspective, a film that would take you 30 minutes to download via broadband today would have taken over six hours on dial-up.

And then there is the fact that it used your actual phone line. Unless you were savvy enough to have more than one line coming into the house, going online meant nobody else could use the phone. This sparked cries of, 'Get off the bloody phone, I need to send some emails!' or 'Get off the bloody internet, I need to call my mother!'

So it is a good thing that we have moved on. It really is. But those of us who heard them shall never forget those squeally plinky plonky noises.

Dodo Rating: 🐤🐤🐤🐤

BASIC

BASIC (the acronym stood for 'Beginner's All-purpose Symbolic Instruction Code') was the most common and popular computer programming language during the rise of the home computer in the late '70s and early '80s. It was simple and clunky, but effective, and, most importantly, quite easy to learn. When schools started teaching Computer Studies around that time, the lessons centred around programming in BASIC.

The language relied upon a range of instructions, many of which were written in longhand and would have made sense to even the most computer-illiterate user. For example, here is a BASIC program that most people will be able to work out.

```
10 PRINT "21st Century Dodos"
20 GOTO 10
RUN
```

If you were to type those lines into your Vic 20 or ZX Spectrum, your screen would be filled with the title of this book over and over again. What fun.

You could, of course, tackle more complex programs, and some of the most popular text adventure games of the time were entirely written in BASIC. However, for more serious gaming you needed specialised code, and as home computing became more about managing fictional football teams and running around tombs with unfeasibly breasted women, and less about two oblongs playing tennis, BASIC became a thing of the past.

At least, it did in its original guise. Ever evolving, BASIC has morphed and changed and can still be seen in the form of Microsoft Visual Basic, which remains a popular language for programmers.

Well, I say popular; it drives a lot of them mad, but it is still around. Not quite extinct yet.

Dodo Rating: 🐤🐤🐤

Compact Discs

Can you remember when compact discs were the future? When the presenter on *Tomorrow's World* tried to prove they wouldn't scratch or jump (which we all now know was a lie but we believed back then)? When you plugged in your first CD player? I bet you can still remember the first CD you ever bought. Mine was *Hello Hello Hello (Petrol)* by Something Happens, a CD single that I purchased a full three months before I had a machine to play it on.

They changed everything. The sound quality was much better than the previously popular cassette (although not as warm and rich as vinyl, as luddites were keen to point out at every available opportunity). They were smaller, so took up less space. They contained more information, so had a longer playing time. There was no A or B side, so bands approached albums very differently, recording songs that were intended to be listened to in a 70(ish)-minute stretch, rather than two 25-minute sessions. The inner sleeve was replaced by the CD booklet. And, although they weren't indestructible and did skip, they were much more durable than tapes or LPs.

During the late '80s and throughout the '90s, music fans spent billions of pounds replacing their old tape and LP collections with new CD versions, which were often remastered with extra tracks. The CD format was seen as the perfect fit for the new albums that came out during that period – albums such as *Brothers in Arms* by Dire Straits, that is widely claimed to be the first million-selling CD, although U2's *The Joshua Tree* is often given that title.

The compact disc itself was invented in the late '70s and was an offshoot of the laserdisc technology of the same period. Both Sony and Philips were working on prototypes, and the first test CD was a recording of Richard Strauss's *Alpine Symphony*. That *Tomorrow's World* demonstration took place in 1981, and the album they played was *Living Eyes* by The Bee Gees which, ironically, is an album that pretty much the whole world has subsequently forgotten including, quite possibly, the brothers Gibb themselves.

The CD went into commercial production in 1982 and the first album to be released on it, rather than an existing album being made available on the format, was *52nd Street* by Billy Joel. Since that time, several billion have been manufactured and sold; 400 million a year at the height of its popularity.

Sadly for a technology with the word 'compact' in its name, the CD is slowly being killed off by digital music. We can now hold our entire music collection on a device about the size of a playing card, whereas we used to require countless CD racks from IKEA to do the same. Even hardened musos are seemingly content to download new albums straight to their iPod or phone, and sales of compact discs are plummeting, with some artists ignoring the format completely. The CD isn't dead, and probably won't be for a fair while given the sheer volume of discs that are out there, but it deserves its place on this endangered list as it is certainly on the decline.

And, somewhere in his huge mansion, Mark Knopfler is softly crying in front of his wall of platinum discs.

Dodo Rating: 🐦🐦

147

Sony Walkman

Now we come to our cover star, the Walkman. If Sony were to invent it today, it would have to be called the Walkperson, but back in the late '70s it was perfectly acceptable to be sexist in a brand name.

The origins of the Walkman are actually very interesting. It was created by a Sony engineer, Nobutoshi Kihara, for his chairman, Akio Morita. Morita was flying all around the world on business, and wanted to be able to listen to his favourite operas while travelling. Kihara created a portable tape player with small headphones – a personal stereo.

Of course, Walkman is actually the Sony brand name, most other manufacturers used 'personal stereo' as a generic term. Although Sony were widely credited with inventing the technology, there was something called a Stereobelt created by a German, Andreas Pavel, in the early '70s, and 30 years later Sony had to settle with him and credit him with founding the device.

But, whoever was responsible, it revolutionised entertainment for years, perhaps forever, with the current digital incarnation of iPods and similar devices all owing a great debt to that first simple idea – 'I want to listen to music on the move, without annoying the people around me.'

Or, 'without annoying them *too much*'. The incessant chhzzchhhzchhhzz of noise bleed from the headphones would gradually drive other people mad, especially on commuter trains and buses. This is still a problem today, but most would consider it a small price to pay in return for music on the go.

The first Walkman was a cassette player and that was the standard device for many years. It did evolve into a CD version – the Discman – and now the digital devices we know today. It was the accessory of choice for joggers and roller skaters throughout the '80s, and paved the way for today's society where everyone goes around with white earbuds and nobody talks to each other any more.

Oh.

I am sure there are still some people who own and use a Walkman in its original cassette form, but they must be few and far between. As is the nature with any cutting-edge technology, it has been overtaken by smaller, better, and cheaper devices. It played its part, but has now been cast aside.

Dodo Rating:

IN THE CINEMA

Where we sat in the dark, snogged,
and ate popcorn ...

National Anthem

Right up until the late 1970s, the national anthem was played at every screening in cinemas up and down the land. Patrons were expected, but not actually forced, to observe the anthem by standing throughout. Originally, it would have been played at the end of the film, but that tended to lead to a frantic rush for the exits while the credits were rolling (if you've ever seen that *Dad's Army* episode, then you'll know what I mean). It was later moved to the beginning so that unpatriotic scallywags would be immediately identifiable by their insistence on staying seated. Cue lots of tutting from older cinema-goers.

I am guessing that the tradition came to an end when the number of people sitting through the anthem far outnumbered those standing to attention. Or perhaps when multiplexes started popping up in out-of-town shopping centres. Or when most people stopped giving a tinker's toss about royalty and the fine heritage of this great nation. Whatever the reason, it doesn't happen any more.

Dodo Rating:

Commissionaires

There was none of this milling round the foyer, buying pic 'n' mix, or playing on arcade games you get nowadays when you visit the cinema, not during the era of black and white films. No back then, if you wanted to see a film, you would queue up outside until just before showtime, when you would be allowed in to buy your ticket and popcorn.

Looking after these queues were commissionaires, often ex-military chaps in peaked caps and uniforms, not unlike a posh hotel doorman. They would keep an eye out for any troublemakers (watch out for those mods and rockers), ensure the queue remained orderly, and field any questions from excited cinema-goers ('When are you going to bloody well let us in?').

The commissionaire was also in charge of the HOUSE FULL sign that would be plonked in front of some unlucky bugger who had arrived late and was too far down the queue to stand a chance of getting in.

Once the show had started, the commissionaire might be called upon to eject some troublesome oiks and he would appear again as the audience left, to ensure that they made their way home in time for him to nip down the pub for a swift pint.

As cinemas changed and owners realised there was more money to be made by getting people inside the foyer as early as possible, the role of the commissionaire became defunct and went the way of lighthouse-keepers.

Dodo Rating: 🐦🐦🐦🐦🐦

Usherettes

Most cinemas would have a number of usherettes (sometimes ushers, but they were usually female) who wore smart uniforms and would look after patrons once they had made it inside.

She would take your ticket, rip it in half, and often thread the portion she kept onto a string (presumably to keep tabs on how many people were inside). She (or one of her fellow usherettes) would show you to your seat with the aid of her trusty torch.

Bear in mind that in the heyday of usherettes most cinema screenings included a newsreel, a supporting feature, and then the main film, so loads of people would roll up once the house lights had gone down, making the usherette's role vital. It always paid to be polite and friendly to your appointed usherette, as she was more likely to place you in good seats. Dare to be rude, or make the wrong remark, and you'd be stuck right up the back in the corner with a restricted view.

During the interval (more on these in a moment), the usherettes would take up position at the end of the aisles in front of the screen, or at the edge of the balcony if you were in the upper tier, sporting a tray that hung from their necks, containing ice cream and other delights. These would be sold to patrons whose shambolic queue would snake up the aisles.

As with many of the other cinema jobs mentioned in this book, the role of the usherette fell foul of the multiplex cinemas, allocated seating, and computer ticketing systems. As films got shorter in length and stopped having intervals, their ice cream selling skills were no longer required, and the role has pretty much died out today, except possibly in a few arthouse cinemas.

Dodo Rating: 🐤🐤🐤🐤

Newsreels

The origin of the name was simple: a newsreel was one reel of film containing news. They originally lasted for about five minutes, and were screened before the main feature at cinemas. The first newsreel in the UK was shown in 1910; it was silent and captions introduced each item. Before the days of television, and indeed mass radio broadcasts, they were the only alternative to newspapers for updates on national and world events, and they proved to be very popular. So much so that some screens, and sometimes whole theatres, were given over to rolling newsreel coverage.

As technology developed, so did the newsreels, adding sound and, eventually, colour. There were a number of different studios providing newsreel coverage, the most famous of which were Pathé, Gaumont, and Movietone. They came into their own when reporting from the First World War, but the height of their popularity was during the 1930s, when they were a staple of every screening at the local picture house, and the classic format – a magazine of news, sport, and popular culture narrated by a pitch-perfect posh bloke – took hold.

The Second World War was a watershed moment for newsreels. They were still seen as a vital source of information from the front, and they did their best to avoid government propaganda, but as a result they were often the bearers of bad news. The newsreel images of the liberation of those in the Nazi concentration camps shocked a nation, and many thought the studios had gone too far, although history considers them as performing a vital service during a time of great turmoil.

Even after television entered most homes, audiences still sat through and enjoyed newsreels, but the writing was on the wall when the BBC introduced live daily news in the mid-'50s, and the cinema version, which only changed twice a week, was seen as dated and out of step.

Remarkably, newsreels continued to be shown in some cinemas throughout the 1960s, and the last company producing them, mainly for overseas screens, closed its doors in 1979.

Subsequently, the newsreel archives have become important historical documents for scholars, and are often plundered for footage by documentary makers. Pathé news issued 'best of' collections taken from every year of broadcasts, as video cassettes, and later DVDs and even multimedia greetings cards, to be given as gifts marking a person's year of birth. So, although you don't see newsreels at the cinema any more, they are still available to view and learn from, for, as we know, history has a habit of repeating itself.

Dodo Rating: 🐤🐤🐤🐤

Smoking Sections

Smoking sections in the cinema used to be on the right-hand side.

Or perhaps that was on the left?

Either way, one half of your local Odeon would permit nicotine addicts to spark up to their heart's content (or until their hearts packed in, whichever came sooner). This was fairly common practice up until the mid-'80s, when most cinema chains phased out smoking areas which, to give them some credit, was about 20 years before the UK government managed to do likewise in other public places.

Those of us who can remember these pro-smoking days recall a strange wall of fog covering 50% of the screen. If you were a non-smoker sitting with a smoker, or had the misfortune to turn up late and find no seats in your half of the theatre, then you had to watch the whole thing through a mist.

This may well have been fine for some films – I am sure that *Howard the Duck* was enhanced by not being able to see much of the actual film – but cinema-goers watching *The Fog* must have been doubly blinded.

Dodo Rating:

Intermissions

Intermissions – a break of five to ten minutes in the middle of a film – were pretty standard cinema practice until the early 1980s, but are an extremely rare thing nowadays.

The intermission served many a purpose. It was a chance for the projectionist to change reels without having to rush around like billy-o to make it appear as seamless as possible. It gave those in the seats time to nip out for a quick wee – these were the days before pelvic floor exercises, you understand. But, most important of all, it offered cinema staff the opportunity to flog you more food and drink – hot dogs, popcorn, some nuts from that Crusader who was always being asked if he had any, or a refreshing Kia-Ora, unless you were a crow as it was, apparently, too orangey for you.

Oh, and let's not forget that films in the old days were *looooong*. Very long.

Consider this. Some of the most popular children's films of the past 20 years or so have been *Toy Story 1, 2*, and *3*. They run for 80, 92, and 103 minutes respectively.

Mary Poppins, on the other hand, lasts for 2 hours and 20 minutes. Can you imagine keeping a kid in a cinema seat for that long without the need for a widdle? It was nigh on impossible without an intermission.

Films for grown-ups were, of course, even longer. *Gone with the Wind* clocks in at just under four hours. *Lawrence of Arabia* is not much shorter. I remember going to see *Gandhi* with my school in 1982 and that definitely had an interval. At 3 hours and 11 minutes, it needed one.

So where did the intermission go – assuming, of course, that a period of nothingness can go anywhere at all – and why don't we have them any more? Films are often still long enough – *Avatar* is pushing three hours and the splendid *Assassination of Jesse James by the Coward Robert Ford* is pretty much the same length (and worth every second, if you ask me) – but we seem to be credited with the ability to sit through them without the need to top up on food or get rid of excess fluids.

There are a number of reasons, and the truth is probably a combination of the lot of them. Very few cinemas actually project film any more, the films being screened digitally or from a DVD, so there is no need to change the reel. The multiplexes that sit next door to multi-storey car parks in out-of-town shopping centres like to show a film a number of times in each screen every day, so the lack of intermission speeds up their turnaround time. And the gigantic portions of food served these days can easily last us three hours, if we pace ourselves.

Intermissions are now very rare and often only used for novelty effect. Quentin Tarantino and Robert Rodriguez's two-part film *Grindhouse* was shown in US cinemas with an intermission between the two, as a homage to the film genre they ripped off – sorry – paid tribute to.

Dodo Rating: 🐦🐦🐦

Waiting Ages for American Films to Come out

There were very practical reasons for this, but it was bloody annoying nonetheless. You see, from the early days of cinema right up to the late 1990s, it was common for UK audiences to have to wait months, sometimes over a year, to see the big new Hollywood films. It was not uncommon in the '70s and '80s for the Oscars to be full of films that no one in the UK had had the chance to see at all. It used to drive film buffs mad.

It was all down to the cost of film stock. In the days of film reels and projectors it cost a lot of money to make each copy, and studios and distributors tended to produce a certain amount for the US markets and then ship out the same stock to their overseas market once the Yanks were finished with them. We were basically getting America's hand-me-downs. It made commercial sense, but it also meant that us lot in Blighty were twiddling our thumbs for months on end waiting for a film to finish its run in the US before we got to see it.

There were other benefits for the film companies from this strategy. If a film absolutely tanked in the US, they could decide not to release it elsewhere at all, thereby saving the cost of distribution and marketing. They could also spread out the promotional campaigns, and not have to squeeze the press junkets into one or two days when the film stars were available.

This practice has pretty much fallen by the wayside now that multiplexes show most films digitally, and there is no need to ship loads of film stock overseas. You do still see a bit of a delay, often to allow actors to travel to the various locations for promotional purposes, but we are now only talking a few weeks at most.

Dodo Rating: 🐦🐦🐦🐦🐦

Local Cinema Adverts

EXT. DAY

*Two animated chaps, both of whom look a bit like that bloke the
Pink Panther spent most of his time pissing off, are running
down a sketchily drawn high street.*

CLOSE UP

CHAP 1: 'Ere Bert, this is the place.

CUT TO

*Dodgy still photograph of an Indian restaurant with shaky text
proclaiming the name of said establishment.*

VOICEOVER: Just a short walk from this theatre.

Ahh, those were the days. No cinema trip was complete without a
flurry of shockingly bad adverts for local shops, businesses, and
eateries. They were usually slotted in after the big budget ads for
Malibu and Cinzano, and before the Crusader was asked if he had
any nuts and the Westlers hot dog appeared from the side of the
screen like a giant penis. Perhaps the thinking was that we wouldn't
notice how terrible they were if they were sneaked in between
proper commercials.

It never worked.

Dodo Rating: 🐤🐤🐤🐤

Saturday Morning Cinema

You would turn up at your local Odeon or ABC cinema at 10am on a Saturday morning, load up on penny chews, and sit down with your mates for two to three hours of uninterrupted viewing pleasure.

The Saturday morning cinema screenings were for kids' films only (with begrudging dads often sitting up the back having a snooze or trying to read the paper from the refracted light of the projector), and were made up of cartoons, adventure serials, public information films, and other odds and sods the projectionist found lying around.

The adventure serials were the best. Flash Gordon would zoom across the screen in pursuit of, or escape from, Ming the Merciless, and every episode would end on a cliffhanger, meaning you had to go back the following week to find out what had happened. These serials kept doing the rounds for decades, with kids of the '70s and early '80s watching black and white shows from the '30s and '40s. No one seemed to mind, but they didn't have Nintendos and mobile phones back in those days.

I seem to remember a serial from the '70s that featured a disembodied head (possibly a shrunken one from a South American tribe?) who hung about with a bunch of kids and got up to all sorts of scrapes. There was a particularly peculiar song at the beginning, with the head singing direct to camera. If anyone else can remember this oddity, then do please drop me an email; the address is at the end of this book.*

Dodo Rating: 🐤🐤🐤🐤

---

* **Update:** *Thanks to everyone who mailed in to inform me that this was Chico the Rainmaker. You can find him on YouTube but, be warned, he is a scary blighter.*

Projectionists

A typical projectionist's job description from 10 or 20 years ago:

> Working alone, in a windowless room, you will be operating a
> number of mechanical projectors and ensuring the smooth
> running of films in each of the cinema's screens. Heavy lifting
> may be required to transport reels from one screen to another.
> You may also be responsible for the physical environment of
> the auditorium – air conditioning, lighting, curtains, etc.

Other responsibilities will include:

- checking film reels as they arrive from distributors
- loading reels, in the right order, onto the projectors
- ensuring the smooth running of each film while playing
- checking sound
- maintenance of equipment
- hours will include afternoons and evenings.

A typical projectionist's job description today:

- Press play

The rise of the multiplex and digital projection means that the art,
and it is an art, of film projection is dying out. Splicing lengths of
film together, setting a new reel up for showing, the intricacies
of the projector itself are all being replaced through the use of hard
drives. One 'projectionist' can now manage every screen in a multiplex from a computer at a desk. Next time you go to see a film, the
chances are there will be no one in the actual projection room
at all.

Ah, but this is progress, I hear some of you cry, and perhaps it is. But it is soulless, heartless, humanless progress and I am not sure I like it.

Dodo Rating: 🐤🐤🐤🐤

B Movies

Or supporting features, to give them their proper name.

These were often, but not always, low-budget films screened before the main attraction or as part of a double-bill. Cinema-goers got more for their money in those days, with several hours of viewing for the price of one ticket. B movies would frequently prove to be the training ground for the stars of tomorrow, with actors such as Robert De Niro, John Wayne, and Jack Nicholson, and also Oscar-winning directors such as Frank Capra, Jonathan Demme, and Francis Ford Coppola, all cutting their millionaire teeth on low-budget supporting features.

Essentially these were films that didn't cost very much to make, relatively speaking, and didn't need a ton of marketing money thrown at them for the simple reason that they were being shown before a film that did have a ton of marketing money thrown at it. They gained most of their audience by default.

This is not to say that they didn't have their fans – far from it. Over the last 60 or 70 years, a massive fanbase for B movies has sprung up, especially the genre films – science fiction, westerns, and particularly horror. Some of the greatest horror films ever made were B movies, or came from B movie beginnings.

B movies started out in the '20s and '30s with studios forcing theatres to take the supporting feature if they wanted to show the big blockbuster. The practice continued for many years, and only really died out in the 1980s because of the sheer cost of production; films that had once cost less than $100,000 to make were now closer to millions. Nothing was really 'low budget' any more.

Dodo Rating:

IN THE NEWSAGENT

Where we bought our sweets and comics …

IN THE NEWSAGENT

Where we bought our sweets and comics...

10p Mix-up Bag

In the 1970s, the ten-pence piece was a magical coin. It was, for most kids, the sum total of their pocket money for the week. It was also the shiny silver key that unlocked the wonders of the mix-up bag.

Whatever you called it where you lived – 10p mix, mix bag, ten penny mix-up – it amounted to the same thing: a small paper bag into which you could place an array of sweets until you reached your budget.

And, magically, ten pence worth of sweets was just enough to get the average child through a suburban Saturday.

All newsagents had a selection of penny sweets in front of their counter. They displayed them there so that they could keep their beady eye on schoolchildren who might be, shall we say, a trifle overzealous with their selections, or those for whom the capitalist notion of fair payment for goods was slightly lower down the pecking order than the thrill of hiding a pink shrimp up your sleeve.

There was a variety of selection methods available. These were very much dependent on the layout of the shop, the trusting/gullible nature of the proprietor, and/or the range of sweets available.

Self-service. A stash of paper bags hung from a string next to the cornucopia of tubs and boxes of sweets. You helped yourself to the sweets you wanted before handing over the bag for payment. This was the most common practice.

Deluxe self-service. As above, but with a small pair of tongs.

Assisted service. Where the newsagent himself would handle the bag and selection process, guided by the juvenile customer. 'I'll have one of them … and one of them … no, hang on … two of them …

how much have I spent so far?' This was a less common approach, and was normally restricted to the particularly friendly proprietor – 'Can I tempt you with some Parma Violets?' Answer: 'No you can't' – or grumpy ones who didn't trust kids to do it themselves. It tended to be unpopular with the adult customer queuing behind waiting to buy 20 JPS and a copy of *Razzle*.

But far more important than the selection method was the selection itself. Which combination of sweets would you go for? There was generally a lot to choose from: Black Jacks, Fruit Salad, liquorice pipes, flying saucers, chocolate rainbow drops, cherry lips, pink shrimp, fried eggs, gobstoppers, Hubba Bubba, golf ball chewing gum, Refresher chews, red bootlaces, coconut mushrooms, aniseed balls, fizzy coke bottles, Mojos, milk bottles – I could go on!

The final decision was a combination of impulse purchase and mental arithmetic. You wanted to get as many sweets as possible for your money, but the real gems on the counter were often that little bit more expensive.

For reasons of clarity and modern comparison, we shall assume that we are talking post-decimalisation currency for this next bit.

In the early to mid-'70s we still had the halfpenny piece, and sweets such as Mojos, Black Jacks, and Fruit Salads were priced at ½ pence each (I am sure I can remember these being two for a ha'penny at some point but perhaps I was imagining that). So you could ram your bag full of 20 halfpenny chews and have enough sugar to keep you going for the whole weekend. Which was fine, but lacked a certain variety.

On the other hand, if you went for too many tuppenny sweets, such as Refresher chews or lollipops, then you could be going home with just five items and lots of empty space in your bag.

So, the best strategy was to include a combination of price points, genres (chews, chocolates, sucky sweets, etc.), and sizes.

It was not an exact science, but it was often possible to exit the sweet hop with the near-perfect selection.

Here is my suggestion for the ideal 10p mix-up bag:

1 x Black Jack	½p
2 x Fruit Salad	1p
1 x Mojo	½p
1 x Swizzle lolly	2p
1 x Hubba Bubba	1p
1 x large pink shrimp	1p
1 x milk bottle	½p
1 x coke bottle	½p
1 x Refresher chew	2p
1 x flying saucer	1p

You can still find mix-up selections in many corner shops and newsagents, but the prices have really shot up, enough to make your eyes water more than a quick shot of lemon sherbet.

Dodo Rating: 🐦🐦🐦🐦

Look-in

La-la-la-la-la *Look-in* (as the jingle went) was a weekly magazine for children. It was the kid brother (not kid sister, casual sexism was alive and well in the '70s) of the *TV Times*. As such, it only featured ITV shows and the stars of them, but managed to include pretty much every iconic character that appealed to children across the network. It included interviews, features, comic strips, quizzes, competitions, and the ubiquitous letters page.

It ran for 23 years from 1971 and original copies are much sought after by nostalgic 40- and 50-somethings. For many years the magazine would sport a painted cover by Italian artist Arnaldo Putzu. His film poster style illustrations of Richard O'Sullivan, Lee Majors, or the cast of *Space 1999* were very much of the time, so as *Look-in* evolved and became more modern it ditched them in favour of photographic covers of pop and film stars.

A typical issue might include 'Bionic Woman', 'Black Beauty' and 'On the Buses' comic strips alongside interviews with Marc Bolan or Mick Robertson from *Magpie*. The *How?* team could show you how to construct a tug boat from bits of old rubbish or there might be a behind-the-scenes feature on *Tiswas*. Ed 'Stewpot' Stewart manned the 'Newsdesk' page (which was presumably written by a journo and then had Stewpot's mug stuck at the top) and a different celebrity would, allegedly, select the letters for the letters page each week.

The magazine was essentially a propaganda rag for ITV, which may seem a bit dodgy now, but this was back in the day when there were only two TV listings magazines – *Radio Times* for BBC and *TV Times* for ITV – and neither could list the other's programmes. So that made it all OK.

Look-in ceased publication in the mid-'90s (I'll be honest, I am surprised it lasted as long as that), but will be remembered most for being around during the golden age of television in the '70s and '80s, and is fondly remembered by many a kid who grew up at the time.

Dodo Rating: 🐦🐦🐦🐦🐦

Sweet Tobacco

It may be hard to believe now, but the thing I am about to describe really did exist. And it was sold to kids.

Strands of coconut, dusted with cocoa powder and sugar, wrapped in a cellophane wallet, and designed to look like a packet of Golden Virginia tobacco.

And it was bloody great.

You would take a pinch, pop it into your mouth, and see how long you could resist before chewing. Once you had scoffed the lot, a damp finger could excavate any last remaining crumbs or grains of sugar from the packet.

Sweet tobacco vanished from our sweet shops once some jobsworth with a bit of clout noticed that encouraging children to purchase anything remotely resembling cigarettes was probably not a great idea. This may be an unpopular view, but I am not aware that the banning of this delicious tobacco-imitating foodstuff has actually led to any decrease in the numbers of smokers.

Unlike candy cigarettes, which simply changed their name to candy sticks and stopped colouring one end in red, sweet tobacco was not able to rebrand itself and smuggle its way back onto the sweet shelf, probably because it looks, well, just like tobacco.

But rejoice, fellow pretend smokers, there are a few select places that you can still get hold of the stuff. It now comes loosely packaged, no more Golden Virginia wrapper, but tastes just the same. It is well worth tracking it down.

And then feeding to your kids.

Dodo Rating: 🐤🐤🐤🐤

Mandy

Mandy was one of many popular comics from the D. C. Thompson stable and was around, in the form of weekly comics and later as an annual, for 40 years from 1967 to 2007, which is quite an impressive run.

In its early days, *Mandy* was primarily a collection of serialised stories, often with recurring characters, taking the form of comic strips and text stories. Many of the plots would be seen as very clichéd and old school nowadays – nurses with a heart of gold, tragic orphans, etc. – and this was definitely no place for boys, but it clearly holds fond memories for many women across two, and possibly three, generations.

After going it alone for nearly 25 years, *Mandy* joined forces with the *Judy* comic in 1991 and they were both subsumed by the bigger, beefier *Bunty* in 1995. *Mandy* annuals continued to be published every year until quite recently, but without a weekly comic to support them, one can only assume they were purchased by original *Mandy* readers for their offspring. Or perhaps purely for nostalgia.

Of course, there is nothing wrong with that.

Dodo Rating: 🐦🐦🐦🐦🐦

Marathon

Packed full of peanuts, and with a solid, dependable name that suggested you could run for 26 miles and a handful of yards on just one bar.

And then it went all international on us and changed its name to Snickers.

Which is just plain silly.

(See also *Jif* and *Opal Fruits*.)

Dodo Rating: 🐤🐤🐤🐤

Opal Fruits

From 1959 to 1998, they were made to make your mouth water.
Since 1998 they have been called Starburst.
Which is just plain silly.
(See also *Marathon* and *Jif*.)

Dodo Rating: 🐥🐥🐥🐥

Playhour

Sonny and Sally of Happy Valley were the stars of *Playhour*, a comic for younger readers that ran from 1954 to 1987. These two happy kids with their little pet lamb featured in a comic strip told in rhyming couplets, just like the original Rupert the Bear annuals, and also replied to any letters sent in by readers.

The rest of the comic was a mixture of original strips such as 'Norman Gnome', 'The Travels of Gulliver Guinea-Pig', and 'Leo the Friendly Lion', as well as stars of the small screen, including *The Magic Roundabout* and *Pinky & Perky*.

Unlike most other comics, *Playhour* avoided the use of speech bubbles in its stories, using captions above or below the panel instead. It also adapted classic children's books in cartoon form, one of the most popular being a version of *Wind in the Willows*.

By the late '80s, the children's magazine market was beginning to be taken over by the big TV franchises such as *Mighty Morphin' Power Rangers* and *Pokemon*, and the somewhat quaint and old-fashioned *Playhour* was removed from newsagents' shelves.

It is an inevitable side effect of our modern culture, I suppose, but it is a shame nonetheless. My own children have seen copies of *Playhour* and other similar comics and annuals, and have enjoyed and devoured them as vigorously as a *Dr Who* magazine. Good storytelling never ages, and *Playhour* certainly had that.

Dodo Rating:

Texan Bars

The Texan is probably the chocolate bar that people get most nostalgic for nowadays; it has become the touchstone retro sweet and memories of it can bring a tear to the eye of grown men and women. Providing that man or woman is over 35 or so, otherwise they won't have clue what a Texan bar is.

It was actually quite a simple confection, nougat and toffee covered in chocolate, but was, as the slogan suggests, somewhat chewy, taking a long to time to finish. A fact that the advertisers made the most of in the commercials. The most famous of which featured a cowboy tied to a stake while a horde of Indians danced around him.

'Hold on there, Bald Eagle', the cowboy says to his captors, 'you wouldn't fire a man till he finished his Texan bar, would you?'

The Indian – or Native American, as I think I should refer to him now – gives a gasp of surprise and/or assent and then the cowboy pipes up again.

'Just bite through the chocolate, and chew. Real slow.'

The Indians keep dancing. The cowboy keeps eating. The Indians wear themselves out and fall asleep. The cowboy prises the stake out of the ground and walks out of the camp, commenting: 'Someone should have told 'em a Texan takes time a-chewin'.'

So there you go, the perfect chocolate bar if you are captured by a hostile tribe and need to bore them to sleep.

The Texan was manufactured throughout the '70s and part of the '80s, but Rowntree's discontinued them for reasons unknown, presumably lack of sales, but given the huge public excitement when they announced their return in 2005, one would have thought there were sales to be had.

Unfortunately, the comeback was for a limited period only; they are once again confined to the shelves of that newsagent in the sky.

I am reliably informed that if you stick a Double Decker in the fridge, wait for the top bit to go hard and then slice off the nougat layer, it does taste a bit like a Texan. I haven't tried it, though.

Dodo Rating: 🐦🐦🐦🐦🐦

Bunty

Bunty was an exception to the overwhelmingly middle-class magazines and comics for girls from the '60s and '70s, in that it went out of its way to appeal to a working-class reader. Characters and strips, such as 'The Comp', set in a comprehensive school, were targeted at just that audience.

And it must have been deemed a success, as it ran as a weekly publication for over 40 years.

Regular features included 'The Four Marys', a cartoon strip set in a boarding school (one of whom was on a scholarship, before you pull me up on the whole working-class thing), two different ballet series, puzzle pages, and a cut-out doll with different outfits.

Bunty absorbed fellow comics *Judy* and *Mandy* in 1995, but the weekly edition moved to a monthly, and in later years there was just a hardback annual at Christmas.

However, having entertained over four decades of girls, there are more than enough mums passing old copies down to their daughters so the tradition kind of lives on.

Dodo Rating: 🐥🐥🐥🐥🐥

Cheeky Weekly

One comic from the '70s that has yet to benefit from a nostalgic reprint is *Cheeky Weekly*. It ran from 1977 to 1980.

Our eponymous hero was a kid with massive teeth who punned his way through every page, often accompanied by a pet snail. Readers were fond of scouring each panel to see if they could spot the snail that was often hidden away in hard-to-find places, a forerunner of *Where's Wally?* perhaps?

Cheeky Weekly was unique among British comics in one major respect: Cheeky himself featured in many strips in each issue, in a sort of linking narrative. Cheeky would get up to some scrapes, make a few jokes (often really cheesy puns), and there would be some tenuous link to the next story.

And what stories they were – classic comic book fare with a few characters that you wouldn't see published today. There was Gunga Jim, an Indian kid with a turban, and Ah-Sew, an Oriental tailor, but also less contentious regulars, such as Herman the traffic warden, Flash Harry the newspaper photographer, and the imaginatively named Butcher Boy who was not, sadly, a graphic interpretation of the Patrick McCabe novel, but was, instead, a boy who worked in a butcher's shop.

Cheeky himself had started out as a character in the strip 'The Krazy Gang' from *Krazy Comic*. He proved so popular with readers that he was soon given his own strip, ''Ello It's Cheeky', but was further promoted to star in his very own comic which ran for three years before merging with *Whoopee!*

Dodo Rating:

Candy Cigarettes

Two types of candy cigarette were common in the UK right up until the mid-1980s, when the powers that be dictated that making cigarettes fun (and tasty to boot) wasn't the best way to discourage children from smoking.

The most popular version was a small chalky sugar stick, with one end coloured red to resemble a lit cigarette. They came in packs of ten or so, with the box itself looking more like a matchbox.

Less common, and also more expensive, were larger chocolate sticks wrapped in paper. The paper was, rather stupidly, inedible and hard to peel off. Even as a seven-year-old, I knew they were missing a trick there – a bit of rice paper would have saved a lot of hassle and avoided the chocolate under fingernail problem. These came in a box about the same size and shape as a packet of fags, and were branded to look as much like cigarettes as possible.

Although it is sad to see any element of one's childhood disappear, it is hard to imagine this concept getting past the planning stage nowadays. Can you imagine the uproar?

Both types of candy are still available, but have wisely changed somewhat to avoid the wrath of parents and health authorities everywhere. In the case of candy cigarettes it was as simple as losing the red end and rebranding as candy sticks. Although whether kids today can actually see the point of them is another matter entirely.

Dodo Rating:

Nestles

OK, so when did Nestles stop being pronounced 'ness-ells' and start being called 'ness-lay'?

This isn't France, you know!

Dodo Rating: 🐤🐤🐤🐤🐤

Nougat

And while we're at it, who decided that we had to say 'noo-gar' instead of 'nuggat'?

Well?

Anyone?

Dodo Rating: 🐦🐦🐦🐦🐦

Look and Learn

I have a particular soft spot for *Look and Learn*, an educational magazine for children that ran from 1962 right through to 1982. I think it is because of the idea that kids would happily pay money for what was essentially a school textbook just because it looked a bit like a comic. The past was a quaint place.

I managed to dig out some old copies to see what sort of articles they featured. Highlights include a history of the Gypsy way of life, including a guide to the signs they would chalk up outside 'friendly' or 'unfriendly' houses, a piece on cut-throat razors, a photographic travelogue on Venice, a look at how chewing gum is made, and a short biography of the Empress Josephine. Can you imagine such a magazine existing today? Most *adults* I know would struggle to get through it.

The articles were all illustrated, and the magazine used a regular group of artists resulting in a house style that looks quite dated now, but seemed perfectly OK at the time. Think school textbook again, with a slight instruction manual influence. I am pretty sure the artists made a few bob on the side by working on the leaflets you'd find in doctors' surgeries.

My favourite section was the 'Penfriends' column, in which kids from across the country described themselves and their interests in a handful of words, and then waited to receive letters from dozens of other children keen to correspond with them. Penfriends were all the rage back then; I discuss them elsewhere in this book.

But the most popular section was undoubtedly 'The Trigan Empire', a science fiction comic strip. The story of an alien culture, it managed to weave all sorts of educational elements into its storylines.

Ultimately it wasn't a lack of interest from readers that brought about *Look and Learn*'s demise, rather, it was the price of paper. It ended up being too expensive to produce, and shut up shop in 1982, although it has resurfaced with an online archive and a 'best of' book version, so the kids of today can discover all about the Greek god Apollo and how tides work.

Dodo Rating: 🐤🐤🐤🐤

Smarties Tubes

In 2005, some bright spark at Nestlé Rowntree decided that, after 68 years, it would be a good idea to ditch the classic cardboard tube packaging of Smarties and replace it with a flimsy hexagonal disgrace that goes all damp when you try to down a few straight into your mouth. The official line was that the six-sided design, known as a 'hexatube' for crying out loud, would appeal more to youngsters and would lead to less spillage, but conspiracy theories abound, such as the suggestion that the new version is a lot cheaper to produce, or that it is easier to recycle.

Whatever the reason, it was wrong, plain wrong.

Original Smarties (and I am coming over all emotional at the mere thought that the kids of today will have no idea what I am talking about) came in a sturdy cylinder with a plastic lid. The lids were in a variety of bright colours and each had a letter of the alphabet embossed in lower-case on the underside.

It was never altogether clear why the letter was there. In later years, the company claimed that they were intended as educational, to encourage kids to learn the alphabet. That may well be true but I cannot remember anyone ever doing such a thing. The lid, and tube, did have other uses, however, most famously in the Smarties Gun Game.

Every day 570,000 tubes of Smarties are manufactured, each containing an average of 48 Smarties, while 307 tubes are eaten every minute in the UK. There appears to be no evidence that the new design improved sales, but it doesn't look as if the classic packaging will ever return.

At least Nestlé Rowntree had the good grace to acknowledge the end of an era. The final 100 cylindrical tubes to come off the production line each contained a commemorative certificate.

Rules for the Smarties Gun Game (for two players):

- Take two tubes of Smarties.
- Eat the Smarties.
- Examine the lids. The person with the letter nearest the start of the alphabet goes first.
- Replace lids.
- Place tubes on a flat surface – a table or arm of a chair are ideal – with the lid pointing away from you.
- Player one then slams a fist down onto the middle of their tube, sending the lid hurtling off into space and, hopefully, across the other side of the room.
- Player two repeats this procedure.
- The winner is the person whose Smarties' lid travels the furthest distance.
- Repeat until your tubes are knackered or your mum announces that 'You could have someone's eye out with that.'

The game could, of course, involve more players. There was even a solo version.

Dodo Rating: 🐤🐤🐤🐤🐤

Smash Hits

Famous for nearly three decades (it ran from 1978 to 2006) of pop music coverage, when *Smash Hits* first started out it was actually a bit more cutting edge. With the age of Stock, Aitken, and Waterman still a long way off, early issues featured Blondie, the Sex Pistols, and even Sham 69. But it really hit its peak in the mid-to-late-'80s when it was all about Duran Duran, and that bloke with the beret who sang that song about an ansaphone that Andy Warhol seemed to like. Although, even then it did keep a token indie page going for some time, just for the weirdos with crimped hair and DM boots.

The magazine contained posters, interviews (often with tongues firmly in cheek), and record reviews, but, for many, the main attraction was the inclusion of lyrics from the most popular songs of the day, most of which seemed to end with the legendary bracketed phrase '(ad lib to fade)'. This was before the days of karaoke and the closest kids would get to *X Factor* was singing into a hairbrush in front of the mirror. No matter how bad they sounded, *Smash Hits* ensured they were word perfect.

If you were an up and coming pop star, *Smash Hits* was the magazine to be in. Sure, there were rivals, with Jonathan King's *No. 1* mag giving it a bit of a scare in the mid-'80s, but *Smash Hits* was always the favourite. Blimey, even Margaret Thatcher consented to an interview, such was its popularity.

Perhaps the most famous journalist to work on *Smash Hits* was Pet Shop Boys frontman Neil Tennant, but it also gave early jobs to Kate Thornton, Miranda Sawyer, Mark Frith (who went on to set up *Heat*), and Mark Ellen (the man behind *Q* and *Mojo*). It was the pre-teen's *NME* and, as the young readers graduated to more serious fare, so did many of the writers. Except for Kate Thornton, who now presents *Loose Women*.

Ironically, the fall of *Smash Hits* was partly blamed on the rise of the BBC's own *Top of the Pops* magazine, a brand that itself became extinct a few years later. However, the internet, mobile phones, and the proliferation of music channels must share part of the blame. Whatever the reason, by the time it folded, circulation was down nearly a million against the heady days of Culture Club and Johnny Hates Jazz. Shattered dreams indeed.

Modern teens can still enjoy the *Smash Hits* pop philosophy by tuning in to the digital radio station or satellite music channel that bears its name, but it is highly likely that they have never heard of the magazine that started it all.

Dodo Rating:

Spangles

Of all the sweets that have been lost to the great litter bin of time, few elicit such fond memories as the humble Spangle. This is surprising really as, despite the name, they weren't really the most spectacular of confections looking, as they did, a bit like a Tunes throat sweet.

Most people remember the distinctive orange packet with the '70s bubble lettering – it was foil, and you would tear it open to reveal the individually cellophane wrapped sweets inside – but Spangles actually date back to the early 1950s.

Effectively just boiled sweets with a bit of a fizzy edge to them, the classic packet contained the following flavours: lemon, lime, pineapple, orange, strawberry, and blackcurrant. But there were a number of variations over the years, with entire packets featuring one flavour, such as tangerine, acid drop, or barley sugar.

There was even an Old English range, which ran for some time, and included cough candy and liquorice among its selection.

Mars stopped making Spangles in the early '80s, but they brought them back to limited success in the mid-'90s. To be honest, I don't think they were really trying all that hard, as the '90s versions only came in two flavours – orange and blackcurrant – so it is no surprise that they vanished again shortly afterwards.

Dodo Rating:

Liquorice Pipes

Famous pipe smokers of the world include Harold Wilson, Monsieur Hulot, Tony Benn. And seven-year-old Steve Stack, walking home from school puffing away on a liquorice pipe.

A thick leathery wad of black liquorice in the shape of a pipe, with a sprinkling of red sugar at the end to suggest the soft glow of burning tobacco, this was actually a sweet that was sold to kids.

To be honest, it was a bit too much liquorice to eat in one go, and it stuck in your teeth for ages afterwards, but the fact that hardly anyone smokes a real pipe any more would suggest that it didn't really encourage the kids of yesteryear to take up the habit.

Dodo Rating:

Maverick Bar

As this is my book I feel I can allow myself a couple of selfish entries. I doubt if many of you can remember the Maverick, but it was my favourite chocolate bar, and if I want to include it, I bloody well can.

The Maverick was Nestlé's answer to the Fuse bar from Cadbury's. It had similar ingredients – raisins, biscuit, and toffee pieces – but was more rough and irregular, where the Fuse was a pretty standard cuboid. The Maverick trumped the Fuse in that it also had a layer of caramel.

It was very nice, so it was. I used to have one every lunchtime.

At least I did from 1997 to 2000, when they were suddenly, and without warning, discontinued. It seems that the combination of patchwork-coloured wrapper and remarkably bland TV ads failed to ignite the desires of our chocoholic nation. I was gutted.

Still am, to be honest.

But this story has a sort of happy ending. Seven years after the demise of the Maverick I was writing my first book, *It Is Just You, Everything's Not Shit*, and was interviewing the nice people at www.aquarterof.com about sweets and snacks, when I happened to mention my sadness at the lack of Mavericks. A few months afterwards I received an email from Sol at A Quarter Of; one of their suppliers had found a decade-old box of Mavericks and she wondered if I wanted a couple. Her husband had tried one the night before and was still alive so she thought it was safe enough.

I jumped at the chance and was stupidly excited when the jiffy bag turned up containing three bars. I got stuck straight in to one of them, sharing pieces with my kids. It was everything I remembered: crunchy, chewy, chocolatey, caramelly, and lovely.

If a little bit stale.

I lived to tell the tale and ate the remaining two bars shortly afterwards. I got a bit emotional when I finished off the last one, knowing that it was the last time I would ever taste my favourite chocolate bar.

Nothing has since managed to take its place. Not even the KitKat Chunky. I shall learn to live with my loss.

Dodo Rating:

ALL THE OTHER STUFF

Where I have plonked everything else …

Post Office Tower Restaurant

The revolving restaurant at the top of the Post Office Tower (now known, of course, as the BT Tower) closed in 1980, partly out of security fears. The IRA had tried to blow it up in the early '70s and it was seen as too high (in both senses) a risk location.

The Top of the Tower restaurant, to give it its proper name, first opened in 1966 and was run by the people behind Butlins Holiday Camps. The main dining area revolved a full 360 degrees, offering an unprecedented view of London. It took 22 minutes to complete a full circuit, which makes it faster than the London Eye.

The menu was proper posh for the time, all in French, and included such delights as *La Darne de Saumon d'Ecosse*, *Le Rumpsteak*, and *Le Gammon Grillé*. Minimum charge was £2.50 and 'patrons having ordered their food and wine may sit and watch the ever-changing view until they choose to leave'.

The original establishment has been closed for over 30 years, but there had been talk of the restaurant re-opening in time for the London Olympics in 2012, with more than one famous celebrity chef rumoured to be taking charge, but BT cancelled any such plans.

Dodo Rating: 🐦🐦🐦🐦🐦

Telegrams

During the 1930s, over 65 million telegrams were being delivered every year, in the UK alone. *Hand* delivered, that is.

Before the days of email, faxes, and mobile phones, a telegram was often the quickest and most confidential way to send urgent information. The sender would write out the message using as few words as possible (they were charged per word), and hand it over to the telegraph officer (usually at the post office), who would send the message via a radio signal (often Morse code) to the office nearest its recipient. There it would be decoded, written out, and given to a delivery boy to hand over personally.

The role of delivery boy was taken very seriously, and there were strict rules about uniform and behaviour. There was even an early morning exercise regime. It was a very responsible job and the older boys even got to ride motorcycles to speed up delivery.

One of the most famous telegrams was sent in 1910, when the captain of a ship sailing to Canada spotted Dr Crippen among his passengers. He got a message to Scotland Yard, who sent a detective on a faster ship to arrest the murderer upon his arrival.

My own favourite telegram was sent by American humorist Robert Benchley when he first visited Venice. It read: 'Streets full of water. Please advise.'

By the 1960s, the volume of telegram traffic had dropped to about 10 million a year, but the service limped on, making a loss, until 1981, when it was taken over by the newly privatised British Telecom and finally put out of its misery. Stop.

Dodo Rating: 🦤🦤🦤🦤🦤

Carbon Copy Paper

Another victim of our digital age. Although you can still come across it from time to time in some form, when a waiter takes your order at a restaurant, for example, the need for carbon copy paper has more or less vanished from our lives.

Every office, and many homes, would have had a stash of the stuff. In case any of you are too young to remember, it was a thin sheet of paper with a coating of ink on one side. It was used, usually when typing, between two blank sheets to create an instant copy of your document. It could also be used for handwritten copies, which was helpful to the waiter taking orders.

It was pretty weird stuff. You had to be careful when handling it to make sure your document didn't end up with 'blue thumb', and its properties, quite literally, wore off with use, but it did the job nicely.

Until, that is, computers came along. Nowadays it is just a matter of clicking SAVE to ensure that a copy of your letter, invoice, or manuscript of yet-to-be-published book [pauses to save document entitled *21st Century Dodos*] is stored forever. Unless your computer crashes, or your hard drive fails, or you encounter the blue screen of death, of course. Carbon copies did have the advantage of being physical things and immune to computer bugs.

Actually, computers are where carbon copy paper lives on, albeit in a virtual sense. Every time you cc someone in on an email, you are, whether you know it or not, creating an electronic carbon copy.

Dodo Rating: 🐦🐦🐦🐦

Concorde

I live near Heathrow airport and twice a day, every day, my house would shake as if there were a small earthquake underfoot, and a noise similar to the one Donkey Kong makes when bashing down the girders (only a lot louder) would drown out all other sound.

If any other plane were responsible for such disturbance, then I'd have written to my MP, complained to the highest authority, and refused to pay my taxes until they fitted a muffler but, somehow, the fact that it was Concorde made it OK – exciting, even. Catching a glimpse of that ivory bird as it flew overhead was a highlight of the day.

It was a peculiar beast in almost every respect. The only commercial plane to fly faster than the speed of sound, it was conceived in the late 1950s when several countries were investigating supersonic transport, including Britain and France. With considerable backing from their respective governments, BAC and Aerospatiale joined forces to work on Concorde, so named to reflect the friendly arrangement that had brought it about.

By the time test flights were taking place in the late 1960s, most of the other countries had dropped out of development, and many had placed orders for Concorde themselves. But even though over 100 orders were taken, a great many were cancelled because of concerns over cost and, in the end, only 20 were manufactured, of which 14 made it into commercial service.

Concorde had looks and it had speed. Its peculiar wing and nose design made it unlike any other aeroplane in the skies, instantly recognisable. It could fly at more than twice the speed of sound (Mach 2.04, 2,173 kph or 1,350 mph) and that meant that it cut hours off long-distance flights. It still holds the record for the fastest transatlantic airliner flight of 2 hours, 52 minutes, and 59 seconds, at an average speed of 1,920.07 kph (1,193.08 mph), which it achieved on 7 February 1996 between JFK and Heathrow airports.

It cost a pretty penny to fly on, though; at least it did once British Airways paid off the government and assumed full ownership in 1983. As a result, passengers tended to be top businessmen (who were charging it on expenses), Hollywood actors, or rock stars.

That wasn't the only drawback. It was, as I mentioned at the beginning, bloody noisy, and several countries refused to allow it to pass through their airspace. By the time of its retirement it was only running a select number of routes.

Quite why the decision was taken to ground the aircraft in 2003 is unclear. British Airways and Air France claimed it was uneconomical to continue flying following a decline in passengers after the (only ever) Concorde crash in 2000, and the 11th September attacks in 2001, but there are suggestions that it was simply more profitable to fly the Concorde routes with traditional subsonic planes.

Whatever the reason, in October 2003 the fleet of Concordes took to the air for a final time. A series of flights around the UK enabled the general public to say farewell to this historic craft. People turned out in their thousands.

There was a last-minute attempt to save the fleet, when Sir Richard Branson offered to buy the planes from BA to re-brand as Virgin. The offer was declined, presumably in part because the two companies loathe each other.

Some of the remaining craft are now on display in museums around the world.

Dodo Rating: 🐦🐦🐦🐦

Passing Back to the Goalie

It used to be a staple part of any football match. With a score 1–0 up, with 15 minutes to play, the defender would pass back to his keeper, who would pick up it and then spend, oh a good two or three minutes standing around until the referee reminded him of the point of the bloody game, and he would throw it back out to that same defender who would dribble it a few yards before hoofing it all the way back again.

It was dull as anything to watch.

So dull, in fact, that in 1992 FIFA brought in a law banning the keeper from handling the ball following a back pass. This was as a direct result of 1.4 billion people falling asleep during the 1990 World Cup Final between Argentina and West Germany. To this day, half of the viewing audience have no idea who won the match.

Dodo Rating:

Football Rattles

It was the iconic image of a football fan – flat cap, knitted striped scarf, and big wooden rattle.

Nowadays, the flat cap has been replaced by a dodgy gelled hairdo, the club scarf is a more elaborate printed affair emblazoned with a logo, but the rattle is rarely to be seen at all.

It did make an unholy racket and I am sure most fans don't miss it, but it does seem odd that something so fundamentally linked to the history of the game simply doesn't appear any more. We can probably blame the hooligans for that; any object that could be used as a weapon is banned from the terraces.

Not that we have terraces any more, either.

The wooden football rattle was actually a modified version of a classic percussion instrument known as a ratchet or noisemaker, and its dulcet tones can be heard in Arnold Schoenberg's *Gurrelieder* and in other compositions. It is a popular instrument in traditional Jewish music, and was also once used by policemen instead of a whistle.

But it is best known in this country as a noisy wooden contraption used to cheer on your team during the big match, sort of a clockwork precursor to the klaxon.

Dodo Rating: 🐦🐦🐦🐦

Typewriters

Literally as I sat down to type this entry for the book (on my trusty laptop), word came through the internet (via Twitter, my main source of up-to-the-minute news these days) that the last typewriter factory on the planet was closing its doors.

Godrej & Boyce shut their plant in India in April 2011 because, quite simply, they aren't getting many orders any more. This is, perhaps, not all that much of a surprise. In fact, it may have been more of a surprise that someone somewhere was still making them at all.

But they were. And now they have stopped.

The origins of the typewriter go back to the early 1700s, when Englishman Henry Mill patented a mechanical writing device, and many similar inventions were created over the proceeding 150 years or so until the Rev. Rasmus Malling-Hansen, a Danish chap, brought the Hansen Writing Ball to market, the first commercially produced typewriter.

Hansen's was probably the first of these contraptions to write faster than a person could with a pen, and so became very successful, with machines still in use in the early 20th century. However, no one person 'invented' the modern typewriter; it came about through trial and error, with many boffins beavering away at their own variations until manufacturers settled upon a standard version by the 1910s.

At the height of their popularity – they were pretty much essential for businesses across the globe – they were selling in their hundreds of millions every year. Smith-Corona sold 12 million machines in the last quarter of 1953 alone. But by the 21st century, global sales had fallen to less than half a million a year.

Despite modern technology and the swanky world of word processing, many writers still insist on typing their work on an old-fashioned typewriter. Bestselling novelists such as John Irving and Paul Auster are famous for their reliance on clunky old keyboards. Auster even wrote a whole book about his typewriter called, unsurprisingly enough, *The Story of my Typewriter*.

Despite their enormous influence on the 20th century, the typewriter is no more. There are plenty in circulation, however, and, as they are pretty chunky bits of machinery, the likelihood is that they will hang around for some time to come.

Dodo Rating: 🐦🐦🐦🐦

Penfriends

Do you remember penfriends?

Before the days of emails, instant messaging, and Twitter, people used to write to each other. Some of these were writing to complete strangers.

There were many magazines, most notably *Look and Learn*, that featured penfriend columns – sort of lonely hearts ads, but without the love interest – in which people, usually kids, would write a few words about themselves and hope to receive letters from other readers. If you were particularly taken by an ad, you would send an introductory letter to the magazine itself and they would pass it on. If you received a reply, then the chances are you would start a correspondence.

Many schools also ran penfriend clubs, often organised by international organisations, which hooked up kids from countries all over the globe.

Of course, most of these epistolary relationships lasted no more than one or two letters, but some went on to become lifelong friendships, or even blossomed into romances that years later led to marriage. How sweet.

Penfriends and penfriend clubs still exist, but they have been somewhat overtaken by modern technology, most of us being happy to fire off an occasional email or to start relationships online.

Dodo Rating: 🐤🐤🐤🐤

Tennent's Lager Can Girls

You know how it is, you are sharing a six pack of beer with a bunch of mates and you lose track of which can belongs to whom, and then you start arguing. Strong words are exchanged, punches are thrown, and before you know it, you are all down the A&E with various bits of a glass coffee table sticking out of your heads.

Some time back in the 1950s, breweries had the bright idea of putting a different picture on each can in a six pack so that drinkers could identify their bevvies by the illustration on the front. But what pictures to go for? How about some attractive ladies? Splendid idea. If you started the evening with Debbie, then you stuck with Debbie all night. Not only did the concept reduce the number of punch-ups, it promoted monogamy.

Of course, some people complained that such images were sexist, but that didn't stop hundreds of women launching their modelling careers on the sides of cans. Nor did it stop millions of men from drinking from them.

Although many companies employed these tactics, the most famous ladies were the Tennent's lager lovelies, all of whom were photographed by Mel Gillies. The last set of lager lovelies featured on cans in 1989.

When I mentioned on Twitter that I was writing this entry, I received an instant response from @lucebrett who can remember playing with the empty cans that her father and his friends had finished with, her 'low-rent Barbies' as she called them. I had no idea they had been put to such uses.

Dodo Rating: 🐦🐦🐦🐦🐦

Countries that No Longer Exist

Pick up any atlas, spin any globe, unfold any map of the world, and chances are that it will be out of date.

Mr Milne, my old history teacher (I have already mentioned him in these pages), used to have a tear in his eye when he told us, 'There was once a day when the sun would never set on the British Empire.' And he would proudly display his old globe with its great swathes of pink, the colour of choice for the many countries Britain somewhat impolitely annexed in days of old. That pink began to vanish like a bad rash following a couple of antihistamine tablets, once these countries claimed their independence.

But independence is not the only reason that countries change their names – revolutions, wars, political upheaval, and unification can all lead to new countries, new flags, and new national anthems.

Let us take a few moments to reflect on the following nations, large and small, that are now confined to the rare postage stamp album of history.

Abyssinia	Austria-Hungary
Basutoland	Bengal
Catalonia	Ceylon
Champa	Corsica*
Czechoslovakia	East Germany
East Pakistan	Gran Colombia
New Granada	North Yemen
Ottoman Empire	Persia
Prussia	Rhodesia
Siam	Sikkim

---

* **Update:** *In response to the handful of emails I have received, yes I know Corsica still exists but it isn't a seperate country anymore. So there!*

South Vietnam	South Yemen
Southwest Africa	Tanganyika
Transjordan	United Republic
Urjanchai Republic	USSR
West Germany	Western Samoa
Yugoslavia	Zaire
Zanzibar	

Dodo Rating: 🐤🐤🐤🐤🐤

English Counties that No Longer Exist

The boundaries of fair England have been fixed and set in stone for hundreds of years. No one really disputes where it ends and Scotland starts, or where Wales actually is. The English may not necessarily want to go there, but do at least know where they are.

The boundaries within England, however, have changed quite a lot over the years. In England, we currently have 48 counties. Most of these have been around for donkey's years but governments have mucked about with them several times, and some counties have been abolished altogether.

Take plucky Avon, for example. It was created as recently as 1974, and was formed by taking bits of Somerset and Gloucestershire and sticking them together with the city of Bristol. But in 1996, it was decided it wasn't needed, everything was put back pretty much where it was before, and no more was said about the matter.

Avon isn't the only county to have been erased from the atlas of time. Cleveland suffered the same fate, being carved out of the North Riding of Yorkshire, also in 1974, only to be abolished and plonked back again sometime later.

Then we have the bizarre merger of Herefordshire and Worcestershire, which were squeezed together to form the single county of Hereford & Worcester (the thinking presumably being that if you took the 'shire' off the end of each they could fit snugly alongside each other). Twenty-odd years later they were amicably divorced, and back the way they were once more.

The same with Humberside. Some bright spark decided it deserved to be its own county until an even brighter spark thought it best to plonk it back as it was. Are you detecting a pattern here?

Interestingly enough, the Royal Mail have often chosen to ignore county changes because they proved too expensive to administer.

The most notable example of this is the postal county of Middlesex. There is no actual county of Middlesex any more; it was swallowed up by Greater London in the '60s, but the region still remains as a distinct postal district.

Dodo Rating: 🦤🦤🦤🦤🦤

Telegrams from the Queen

We still refer to a centenarian as receiving 'a telegram from the Queen', even though the old dear hasn't telegrammed anyone since 1981, when telegrams themselves ceased to be issued in the UK.

Since then, Her Majesty has resorted to sending a more traditional card, although these no longer come automatically on your birthday. Someone, presumably a relative, as you are too busy watching *Countdown* and trying to remember the names of your 24 great-grandchildren, has to apply in advance to ensure that you get the special greeting.

It is not only those of us who reach 100 who get a card from the Queen. If you live to 105, then you get another one, and then they keep coming every year till you pop your clogs. She also sends out messages to couples celebrating their 60th wedding anniversaries. Likewise, 70th and 80th anniversaries are also marked in this way.

The reason that the messages are no longer sent out automatically is quite simple – we are all living longer, and it just became too big a job to manage. Less than 3,000 telegrams were sent in the year that Elizabeth II ascended to the throne, but by 2007 there were nearly 8,500 100th birthdays alone, plus over 26,000 diamond anniversaries.

Similar traditions exist in other countries. Centenarians in the US receive a letter from the president, and in Japan they get a silver cup. But the best gift of all goes to any Irish citizens who manage to reach their 100th birthday – they get sent just over €2,500 from the president, even if they no longer live in Ireland.

I hope they blow it all on cheap booze and a night down the bingo.

Dodo Rating: 🐦🐦🐦

214

Lighthouse-keepers

While there are still a small number of manned lighthouses around the globe, the last British lighthouse-keeper handed in his keys in 1998. It is one of the first professions to become completely extinct in this country. Think about it, there are still a few coopers and blacksmiths, and possibly one or two jesters, around. Apart from executioners, I am struggling to think of another job that has completely vanished in this way.

Lighthouses would usually be manned by three keepers, often living on site for months at a time. Their job was to keep the light working – polishing the lens, trimming the wick (before the days of electricity), and other routine maintenance – at all times. Chores would be shared among the men, rotating responsibilities each day. Some lighthouses were on the mainland, and it was possible to leave them to replenish supplies as and when needed, but many were on rocks and islands out to sea, and keepers were stuck there until the next crew arrived, often two months later.

Many of the original lighthouses are still in operation, but are now automated and only require occasional maintenance – there is no need for anyone to live on site. Some of the decommissioned lighthouses have become holiday homes, or museums that are open to the public.

North Foreland lighthouse in Kent was the last one to become automated, over ten years ago.

Dodo Rating:

215

Pipe Smoking

Perhaps the clearest indication of the decline of pipe smoking is a quick look through the winners of the 'Pipe Smoker of the Year' award across the ages.

1965 Harold Wilson

Even though I am too young to remember Wilson's time as Prime Minister (I was a toddler during his second term in the '70s), even I instantly associate him with a pipe. Of the first 20 results on a Google image search for his name, 17 feature Wilson with one in his mouth. In several of them he is puffing away and emitting a plume of smoke. Can you imagine such a thing today – Tony Blair or David Cameron smoking a pipe in the middle of an interview? Come to think of it, it would be pretty awesome, wouldn't it? In 1976 he won the award again, this time named Pipe Smoker of the Decade.

1968 Peter Cushing

Vanquisher of vampires, saviour of big-breasted Hammer damsels in distress, one of the finest Sherlock Holmes to appear on screen, and he was even Dr Who in the film version of the TV show. A proper English gentleman, and pipe smoker.

1969 Jack Hargreaves

Old bloke presenting programmes about country life from a shed. Smoking a pipe in nearly every piece of footage he filmed.

1970 Eric Morecambe

Comedy legend.

1973 Frank Muir

A huge hero of mine and, alongside Denis Norden, half of one of the most successful comedy writing teams of all time. He was also the longest running team captain on *Call My Bluff*. Again, archetypal English pipe smoker, and gent.

1974 Fred Trueman

Cricketing legend.

1983 Patrick Moore

Monocled nutty astronomer, and closet xylophone genius, of considerable size. Again, a classic pipe smoker.

1986 David Bryant

For those who don't remember David Bryant, he was one of the country's leading bowls players in an age when bowls was frequently shown on television and would garner a considerable viewing audience. He played every game with a pipe in his mouth. Later on, rules and regulations banned him from smoking while playing. He then played with an empty pipe in his mouth.

1992 Tony Benn

In what I consider to be the final great year of the award, it was given to a man who must have wondered what he had done wrong in the previous 30 years not to have won it before. Another politician permanently associated with the pipe, he saw his rival Harold Wilson win it twice, decades before he was finally given the prize.

At this point things started to go a bit wrong. It would be easy to suggest that pipe smoking had gone out of fashion, but I am not sure it had ever really been in fashion. You could also point to the increasing concerns about tobacco and health, although I would argue that pipes, although clearly not good for you, never quite had the doctors and health experts as up in arms as cigarettes. Perhaps this was because 14-year-old-kids were rarely nipping behind the bike sheds for a quick puff on a pipe. Whatever the reason, pipe smoking seems to have gone downhill after Anthony Wedgwood Benn picked up his award in 1992.

Don't believe me? Then allow me to introduce the winner of the 1993 award.

Step forward Rod Hull, a man who spent most of his career with his hand up a bird's arse.

And the list of winners since then has rarely reached the dizzy heights of the '60s, '70s and '80s including, as they do, bearded West Country comedian Jethro and Cooperman himself, Russ Abbot. Nothing against these mildly amusing men, but neither of them is exactly Eric Morecambe, are they?

The final winner of Pipe Smoker of the Year was Stephen Fry. Now, there are lots of things you can say about Stephen Fry, plenty of accolades you can bestow upon him, numerous great achievements you can associate him with, but how many of you have seen him with a pipe? Me neither.

That was back in 2003. The award was discontinued at that point because of fears that it would fall foul of the new advertising regulations regarding smoking and tobacco. If this has led to a decline in smoking, then that is surely a good thing, but I, for one, do miss the sight of an old man, in a tweed suit, lighting his pipe in a shop doorway.

Dodo Rating: 🐤🐤🐤🐤

Chest Expanders

Technically they still exist. I looked one up on Amazon just before typing this entry, but let's be honest, when is the last time you saw one advertised, let alone someone actually using one?

Before the days of gym membership and personal trainers, most fitness regimes involved a bit of jogging, an exercise bike in the bedroom, some dumbbell weights, and a chest expander (for the men, not as popular with women).

Chest expanders were/are bizarre things. Four long springs running parallel to each other and connected by handles at each end. The idea was take a handle in each hand, pull in opposite directions, and stretch the springs, thereby giving your pectoral muscles a bit of a workout.

Which was fine, and they worked, but woe betide anyone who exercised without a T-shirt on, when those springs sprang back. Especially gentlemen of a more hirsute persuasion.

It bloody hurt.

You may also remember the Bullworker. A thick telescopic tube with grips at both ends that you squashed together to create a similar rippling torso.

If you cast your mind further back, you'll recall the Charles Atlas ads in the back of comics and magazines for men.

One glance at the physique of the average bloke over 40 and you'll be in no doubt as to how effective these items were.

Dodo Rating: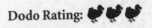

Handwritten Letters

Dear Reader,

I hope this finds you well. I thought I would write you a letter by hand seeing as no one seems to do that these days.

So far this week I have received quite a lot of mail through my letterbox: bills, brochures, a book from Amazon, junk mail and one postcard.

But no letters.

And yet we still call them 'letterboxes'.

Perhaps we should all make the effort to take some time out of our busy lives and write just one letter a month to someone who would appreciate it. A parent or grandparent, a child away at university, a friend we haven't seen for a while, the people in your own home.

I bet if everyone who bought this book sent one, just one, handwritten letter in the next few weeks then the world would be a happier place.

There would certainly be more smiles going around, and that would make it all worthwhile.

Anyway, ponder on that, won't you?

Best wishes,

Steve Stack

P.S. Thanks for buying my book!

Dodo Rating: 🐦🐦🐦

Football Pools

When I was growing up, every Thursday night at my house would be punctuated by a rap at the door as the pools collector came knocking to collect that week's entry.

The football pools were the closest this country had to a national lottery before the days of Camelot and their colourful balls. Millions of people paid an entry fee and tried to predict which eight matches from the coming Saturday's football fixture list would end in a score draw. Points were allocated depending upon the result, typically 3 points for a score draw, 2 for a no-score draw, 1½ points for an away win, and 1 point for a home win. So the maximum you could score was 24.

Each week the person or persons with the highest score would receive a cash prize, known as a dividend. This was often a healthy six-figure sum, but did occasionally top the million pound mark. Essentially, the entry fees from all players were totalled up, a chunk taken by the pools company, then the rest handed out as prizes.

The football pools started out in the 1920s, and the main companies offering the competition were Littlewoods, Vernons, and Zetters. They got round the strict gambling laws because they were classed as a game of skill, rather than chance. The companies employed collectors to call on people's houses and pick up completed forms.

The forms themselves were long grid affairs, precursors to Excel spreadsheet perhaps, with a list of fixtures down the left-hand side (starting with the First Division and running all the way down to the Scottish Second) and a number of columns for multiple entries. The cost per line was often just a few pence, or even a fraction of a penny, but most players entered several permutations, or perms, every week. I remember the form and a few silver coins being left by the front door for the pools collector each week.

When BBC's *Grandstand* broadcast the football results every Saturday afternoon, it included the pools score (3, 2, 1½, or 1) and would show a 'pools forecast', essentially a prediction of the likelihood of a jackpot. If there were only 8 or 9 score draws in any given week, then the jackpot chances were high, 15 or more and it was likely that many people would have a decent points total, so the chances of a big payout were low.

In the off-season, when British teams were having a much-needed break, the pools did not stop. Instead they switched to Australian football matches. This really did make it a game of pure chance. While many players could look at the British fixture list and do their best to predict games in which a draw was the likely outcome, hardly anyone knew anything about the Australian teams, so you just had to take a punt.

The competition still exists today, the three major companies having pooled together (sorry!) to form one online company. This was in response to the launch of the National Lottery in 1994. And, while they are still quite popular, they clearly do not have the national reach that they once had, and the role of the pools collector is long since defunct.

I checked with my dad while writing this entry, and he reckons he played the pools every week for 20 years, and won about £58.

Dodo Rating: 🐥🐥🐥

Spot the Ball

Often run by the same companies as the football pools, but also very popular with newspapers, Spot the Ball was a competition in which a photograph of a football match had been doctored to remove the actual ball. Entrants had to place a series of crosses on the photo in an attempt to predict where the ball was located. The position of the football players, their line of sight, and the direction of the crowd's watchful gaze were all clues as to the ball's real whereabouts. Your entry fee was linked to the number of crosses you placed.

Oddly, the winner was not always the person who got closest to the ball's real location as, due to some quirk of the gambling laws, you couldn't bet on an event that had already taken place, so a panel of 'experts' would select the winning location.

All sounds like a fix if you ask me, but then I am probably just miffed as I never won one.

Spot the Ball still goes on, but it is rather harder to find than it once was.

Pun intended.

Dodo Rating: 🐤🐤🐤🐤

Imperial Measurements

The death knell for imperial measurements sounded in 1995, when the government introduced the Unit of Measurement Regulations Act, which declared that all tradesmen must use measuring devices that included metric quantities. Contrary to popular belief, this did not outlaw imperial measurements, but it did mark an official move from feet and pounds to metres and kilos.

Which, given that this is how the rest of the world rolls, is probably fair enough, but it does ignore the fact that imperial measurements were and are, well, far more common sense than metric ones.

Take the inch, for example. An inch is more or less the length from the tip of a grown man's thumb to his first knuckle. Most men have at least one thumb, often two, and thereby have the means to measure an inch at any time or in any place. It is a very practical measurement, and I am sure it is no coincidence that the words for 'thumb' and 'inch' in languages such as French, Spanish, and many others are the same or very similar.

A centimetre, on the other hand, is one hundredth of a metre, with no sensible or obvious comparison in the real world.

Twelve inches, as every schoolchild knows, make a foot. And that is another eminently practical unit of measurement being, as it is, based on the length of a man's foot.

Three feet make a yard, which is also pretty much the length from the tip of your nose to your thumb, and when merchants of old were selling fabric or material they would measure it by holding it up to their face and stretching it across their extended arm.

The yard's rough metric equivalent is the metre which is, wait for it, the distance light travels in a vacuum in 1/299,792,458 of a second. Practical, huh? To be completely fair, it was originally supposed to be one ten millionth of the distance from the equator to the North Pole, which is a much easier measurement for the ordinary man to check!

Imperial measurements are full of sensible units:

- An acre is the amount of land one man could plough with one ox in one day.
- A stone is roughly the weight of the largest rock a man could comfortably hold in one hand.
- A mile is about 1,000 paces.

While the metric system has taken over, being the legal and official measurement of all trade, the imperial measurements are still clinging on to many aspects of our lives. We still measure distance on our roads in miles, and speed in mph. Most people weigh themselves in stones and pounds. Farmers and landowners still refer to how many acres they own.

And things are likely to stay that way for some time to come. Imperial measurements certainly deserve to be on the endangered list, bureaucracy has seen to that, but their simplicity and practicality should mean that they live on for a while yet.

Dodo Rating:

226

Net Cord Judges

Professional tennis matches used to have a person sitting in front of the umpire's chair with one finger and an ear pressed to the net, listening out for any contact between ball and net cord during the serve. Their cry of 'Let!' signalled the need for a second service.

This is another of those jobs that has vanished off the face of the earth, but most people don't seem to have noticed. If they were reinstated tomorrow, you wouldn't be able to miss them, but their absence seems unremarkable today.

It was possibly the most dangerous job on the tennis court. Sure, you got to sit down all day, were only needed for the first stroke of every point, and could eavesdrop on the mutterings of the players as they changed ends, but you were frequently on the receiving end of a tennis ball to the side of the head. Which would hurt. A lot.

Net cord judges were replaced by electronic devices across the ATP World Tour in 1996, and by the four Grand Slam events shortly afterwards.

They are now well and truly extinct.

Dodo Rating: 🐤🐤🐤🐤🐤

Car Chokes

I'll be honest, as a non-driver I really don't understand what a choke does to a car engine. Even after researching the subject, I am not really any the wiser.

As far as I can ascertain, it controls the ratio of fuel to air that enters the engine. When the car is cold and you need to start it up, the choke helps to reduce the amount of air getting in and (in theory) allows you to start the car without difficulty.

This used to be a manual process. When starting up many cars manufactured in the last century, you would have to pull the choke out – a button or lever on the dashboard – and then gradually let it back in as you made your way along the road. Release it too early and the car could stall.

Nowadays, most vehicles have automatic chokes and young drivers are none the wiser as to their existence. They just turn the car on and drive off.

Such youth won't even remember the days when you had to run in a new engine. A handwritten sign would go up in the back of the car saying something like 'RUNNING IN ENGINE, PLEASE PASS', to avoid getting beeped at for going so slow. You would have to keep the engine below a certain number of revs for the first few hundred miles. For most drivers, it was a flash forward to how they'd be driving when they hit their 60s.

But again, modern technology means that this sort of tortoise like behaviour is no longer necessary, and pretty soon we'll have all forgotten it ever happened.

Dodo Rating: 🐦🐦🐦🐦

Two Spaces after a Full Stop

Many of us were taught to put two spaces after a full stop when typing any sort of document. At least, we were if we grew up in the day when typewriters proliferated, but this is no longer the case. Actually, it wasn't the case before typewriters, either.

Typographers of old went to great lengths to ensure that the printed word was crisp, clear, and readable. To achieve this, they developed a system of proportional type where wide letters took up more space than thin letters, reflecting the way they tended to look when written down by hand.

Then typewriters came along and really buggered things up. You see, manual typewriters use monospaced type in which every letter and symbol is the same width. This is vital to ensure that they actually work and the keys don't stick all the time, but one side effect was that you needed to leave two spaces after a full stop for anyone to actually notice it was there.

The need for monospaced type died out in the 1970s when computers and electric typewriters invaded the office space. Proportional type was restored.

But generations of people had grown up with the two space rule, and it proliferates to this day, albeit in dwindling numbers. It simply isn't needed any more.

Dodo Rating: 🐤🐤🐤

The Word 'Wireless'

When radio first entered people's homes in the 1920s, it was a technological marvel, and the machines used to receive radio broadcasts were given a very modern-sounding name: the 'wireless'. It received signals through the air, you see, the music and talk and sound didn't travel along wires. It was a bit like magic.

But, as technology improved and players became smaller and more portable, the wonder started to wane, and no one really thought the whole wireless thing was a big deal any more. And anyway, 'radio' sounded far more modern. So 'wireless' was used as a term of endearment, a quaint old-fashioned way of saying 'radio'.

But then, almost without anyone noticing, the word 'wireless' became cutting edge again. Everyone and his donkey are emailing, tweeting, blogging, and browsing using wireless technology. The word is back, and looks like it is here to stay.

Which is all well and good, but it does mean that you can't really say, 'Shall we have a listen to the wireless?' or 'I wonder if the United match is on the wireless this afternoon?' without youngsters looking at you as if you are insane.

The word may live on, but its original meaning is all but lost. I think that is rather sad.

Dodo Rating: 🐦🐦🐦🐦

Coins and Notes

I was born in 1970, so the first pocket money I ever received (some years later) was most certainly decimal, but mixed in there was the odd coin from the pre-decimal days, still in use under a new denomination.

Take the shilling, for example, the staple coin of the realm before the 1970s. This carried on being legal tender, but was now worth 5p. I remember the coat of arms on one side and the young Queen's head on the other. Many was the time I would wander down to the corner shop with two of them in my pocket ready to purchase a 10p mix-up bag. The florin was frequently used as a 10p piece itself. Halcyon days.

Not every coin survived the move to decimal, however, even though examples could be found in charity collection boxes and down the backs of sofas for years afterwards. These were the crown, half crown, and threepenny bit. The only exception was the sixpence, which was worth 2½p and carried on till 1980, although by then they were few and far between.

I particularly recall the novelty of coming across a threepenny bit, with its weird 12-sided configuration, and the farthing, which was worth a quarter of a penny and had a wren on the side. We couldn't spend them, of course, but that didn't seem to matter.

But not all the decimal coins survived, either. My kids are dumb-founded by the concept of a halfpenny, so much so that I daren't tell them about the farthing. 'But what could you buy with it?' they ask, and I tell them, 'A Black Jack or a Mojo.' But lots of prices included the halfpenny in the 1970s, it was not uncommon to pay 12½p for a can of something at the supermarket, and few shopping trips were carried out without some ha'pennies in the change.

The halfpence piece was phased out in 1984, and some of the other coins were resized. Ten-pence pieces used to be big blighters, and the five pence was also a lot larger back then, so much so that the introduction of the microscopic versions we have now caused much consternation at the time.

But not as much as the withdrawal of the one pound note, which happened the same year. Having been around for 150 years, it was replaced by the pound coin.

Of course, we all move on, and once a coin or note ceases to be legal tender, it quickly vanishes from circulation, confined to the collections of a few enthusiasts or the junk drawers of elderly grandparents. Still, that doesn't mean we don't have fond memories of the coins we grew up with, the coins in our first week's pocket money, the coins we bought our sweets and crisps with.

Dodo Rating:

READER'S DODOS

Sago

Not the sago we can buy now in the supermarket, which is white and looks a bit like sperm, and tastes like soggy cardboard. When I was a child we had yellow sago, and it looked like yellow frogspawn but tasted sweet and wonderful and was just the very best thing to eat when you had mumps.

Jo Carroll

Guess Who? Characters

I'm always a little sad over things that still exist but used to be so much cooler. Like the characters in *Guess Who?* My brother used to play a version where, instead of asking about their physical characteristics, you'd ask about their lives; for example "would your person spend more to get a genuine leather sofa instead of imitation?" You can't do that with the new *Guess Who?* because the characters are so void of personality.

Janina Matthewson

Itsy & Bitsy

Itsy and Bity, the hand puppet spiders.

Mike

Steve says: Itsy and Bitsy appeared alongside Susan Stranks for 182 episodes of the ITV children's show Paperplay. Itsy was yellow, and a girl. Bitsy was orange, and a boy. Bitsy would often muck around and almost spoil whatever craft creation Susan was attempting to make. They were created and performed by puppeteer Norman Beardsley. You can find clips of the two little arachnoid scamps on YouTube and there was even a range of nostalgic merchandise available some years back.

Nutty Bar

What about the 'Nutty Bar' remember that one? Log shaped – fudgey on the inside, nutty on the outside and reminiscent of a week old, dehydrated turd. I used to love those :-)

Abi Laing

Bubble Cars

Bubble cars had their moment because of the shortages of raw materials in the years following the end of World War II, and the high cost of oil during the Suez crisis of 1956. They were practical, economical, but also really, really cute. They were called bubble cars because the early ones, like the Messerschmitt, had a bubble cockpit-style canopy. Our first 'family' car was a turquoise BMW600 (a 4-seater, 4-wheeled version of the teeny 3-wheeled Isetta), bought second-hand in 1970. It made people stop and stare, especially when it was loaded up for our annual camping holiday: roof-rack on top, a custom-made trailer on the back, five of us plus two dogs crammed inside. No wonder we always broke down about an hour from home. The driver had to open up the front – steering wheel and all – to get in. The engine was under the back seat. The modern equivalent of the bubble car is the Smart car, but aesthetically it has nowhere near the same charm.

Wendy Varley

Cadbury's Creme Eggs

Cadbury's Creme Eggs – the old school ones that were larger and more chocolatey and not so sickly sweet. I'm sure the yolks were brighter and if you took them from the fridge, a sheen of sweat would bloom on their crisp chocolatey shells.

Periwinkle Jones

Watt & Grant Bookshop

Wouldn't mean anything if you don't live in Aberdeen but I miss the book shop in the Watt & Grant department store that was on Union Street.

Annette

Steve says: Watt & Grant traded under that name, although through various owners, from 1927–1953. In its final years it was owned by House of Fraser.

Fish 'n' Chips

Fish 'n' Chips pretend crisps (baked biscuit snack) highly flavoured with salt & vinegar. Flavour disappeared in seconds.

Rusty McGee

Penny Arrow Bar

The Penny Arrow Bar should get a special mention. For a start it was 1p, a bargain by today's standards and it helped many a child get by during desperate pangs of hunger in the run up to dinner. It came in chewy spearmint and toffee flavours too and was so chewy it'd get stuck right between the teeth.

Lloyd Paige

Cresta Pop

Two things (do they all have to be food, by the way?) Cresta pop. I have very vague memories of it. There was a bear involved somewhere and as far as I recall the drink itself had no recognisable taste. Alan Class comics. I seemed to buy these almost exclusively at seaside locations in the 70s and early 80s. They were squarebound reprints of old American science fiction and horror short comics and always remind me of summer holidays.

David Barnett

Afternoon Closedown

You quite rightly included the closedown in your book but you neglected to mention the afternoon closedown. When I was a lad television channels would shut down in the middle of the afternoon. I seem to recall that this was so that kids could do their homework after returning from school without being distracted by the idiot's lantern, but that might have just been an urban myth. Anyway, they stopped doing it in the early 80s and I rarely meet anyone who can remember it now.

John Dinkings

Children's Programmes on BBC1

I was sad to hear that the BBC are to stop showing any children's programmes on BBC1 or BBC2 with classics such as Blue Peter now appearing on CBBC only. A real shame and I think it will have a long-lasting effect on popular culture.

Jack Hardy

Top of the Pops

How's about an entry on Top of the Pops? Or those little LCD handheld game things Nintendo did?

Nik Perring

BBC Television Centre

Just watched an amazing programme about BBC Television Centre. I can't believe that it is being sold off.

Thom Everly

Steve says: BBC TV Centre can, at time of writing, be found in White City in West London. I say 'at time of writing' because the BBC has announced that it will close down in 2013 and stop being used as the corporations headquarters and main studio facility. It won't vanish completely as parts have Grade II listed status but its wonderful position at the centre of great British television is destined to become a thing of the past.

PK Chewing Gum

I always thought I was Dodoless but then realised that once every couple of months I spend a few hours weeping and trawling the internet for PK Gum. My mum always had the licorice and I had the arrowmint and it was my favourite thing ever and then it just disappeared and it ruined my life.

Corinna Harrod

Steve says: I remember my grandmother reciting a poem about PK that went something like this: 'PK chewing gum / a penny a packet / first you chew it / then you crack it / then you stick it to your jacket / PK chewing gum / a penny a packet'.

Fry's Chocolate Fruit Creams

My dodo is the delicious Fry's Chocolate Fruit Creams bar. I always loved the fact that, unlike the tasty but very plain mint version which contains only white fondant, this had a different colour and flavour in each segment, and when you broke of one segment you couldn't avoid get a small teasing taster of the next along too. Ah, such fond memories!

Gina Brown

Steve says: The bar in question actually had two different names (although it was essentially the same thing). Fry's Five Centres was produced from 1934 to 1992 and contained pineapple, lime, strawberry, raspberry and orange flavours. It was withdrawn for a short while in the 60s and rebranded as Fry's Fruit Medley but the Five Centres name soon came back.

The Raggy Dolls

I just wanted to tell you about an old TV program I used to love. It was *The Raggy Dolls* and I haven't seen it for years but me and my best friend would watch it after school. I can still remember the theme tune.

Laura McCormick

Steve says: The Raggy Dolls was created by Melvyn Jacobson and narrated by Neil Innes. It featured the adventures of a bunch of dolls from the reject bin of a toy factory and ran for nearly ten years from 1986.

The End?

So there you have it, an endangered list of 134 inanimate objects (and other things). Some are well and truly extinct, others are just moments away from disappearing, a few showing signs of a comeback.

But does any of this matter? Should we care?

Well, yes and no.

Mankind's eternal quest for progress leaves devastation in its wake. It is the price we pay. I may look back with fondness on the days of teletext and half-day closing, but they are never going to return and, if I am honest, I probably wouldn't swap my internet and 24-hour shopping for them if you made me the offer.

This book was never really about trying to save these things, although it might be nice if we wrote a few more letters to each other and Rowntree's could make some Maverick bars just for me. Instead, I wanted to say cheerio to some important, and other less important, cultural icons, and share with you this fond farewell.

I hope I triggered a few memories by doing so.

Further Reading

If any of the entries in this book have tickled your fancy and given you the notion to read a bit more about them, then here are a few books and websites that I would recommend you check out:

Books

Paul Auster, *The Story of my Typewriter* (DAP, 9781891024320).
  A beautiful collection of words and drawings. A love letter from this remarkable novelist to the machine he uses to write all of his books.
Steve Berry, *TV Cream Toys* (Friday Project, 9781905548279).
  A nostalgia overload in this cracking coffee table book packed full of the toys we all grew up with. You are guaranteed to find dozens of toys and games that you had completely forgotten existed.
Steve Berry and Phil Norman, *The Great British Tuck Shop* (Friday Project 9781906321451). More hardcore nostalgia, this time looking at the sweets, crisps, biscuits, fizzy pop, and ice lollies of yesteryear.
Warwick Cairns, *About the Size of It* (Pan 9780330450300).
  A splendidly entertaining history of imperial measurements.

Warwick Cairns, *How to Live Dangerously* (Macmillan, 9780230712218). The finest argument you will ever read about why you should let your kids climb trees, play in the street, and generally be a bit more reckless.

Graham Kibble-White, *Look-in: The Best of the Seventies* (Prion, 9781853756221). An annual-style collection of the best bits from the heyday of *Look-in* magazine.

Thurston Moore, *Mix Tape: The Art of Cassette Culture* (Universe Publishing, 9780789311993). A collection of handwritten liner notes from old mixtapes, some great works of art among them. Well worth a flick through. It will bring back lots of memories.

I can also highly recommend spending an hour or so and a few quid on eBay to buy up a few comics or annuals that you remember from your youth, especially if you have kids yourself. My two have loved reading the old *Cheeky* annuals I picked up while researching this book.

Websites

likepunkneverhappened.blogspot.com – An online archive of *Smash Hits* covers and articles.

www.aquarterof.co.uk – Online sweet shop that has pretty much everything you can remember from your youth.

www.lookandlearn.com – An online library of pictures and articles from *Look and Learn* magazine's long history.

www.measuringworth.com – A very handy site if you want to find out what £1 in 1970 would be worth in today's money. Or any other value in any other year.

www.tvcream.co.uk – The home of all the TV trivia and nostalgia you could possibly need.

Thank You

A big thank you to everyone who got in touch following the publication of the hardback edition of this book. It was wonderful to hear from so many people who, like me, remember certain inanimate objects with fondness. You can stop sending photos of white dog poo now, though.

I am grateful to all the bloggers who hosted me on my blog tour and to every reader who has reviewed or recommended the book online.

The contributors to the Readers' Dodos section have helped me flesh out this paperback. They did so without payment except for a credit and a free copy of the book. The mugs.

Thanks to Steven Poole in the Guardian for pointing out that I don't know what the phrase 'to coin a phrase means'. Bigger thanks to Jen Campbell and Ben Hatch for agreeing to rave about the book on the cover.

21st Century Dodos wouldn't look the way it does without Corinna Harrod to pull it all together, Jo Walker who designed the cover and Dave Cornmell who drew the illustrations. They are lovely people, and two of them are also very attractive.

Finally, special thanks to some people who helped me out while I was writing the bloody thing:

The readers of my own blog, *Me and My Big Mouth*, who came up with all sorts of ideas for the book throughout its creation.

Kat Stephen, whose expert knowledge on peculiar Scottish beverages was most helpful, I am glad you didn't end up on a ship in the middle of ocean.

Sam McColl, who lent me her cabin in the woods in which to write, largely undisturbed.

And my family, who were very patient and tolerant while I became obsessed with rotary dial telephones, Ceefax and Spangles.

About the Author

Steve Stack is the pseudonym of a blogger and sometime journalist. He is the author of one previous book, *It Is Just You, Everything's Not Shit* which can probably still be found in bargain bookshops and Poundland if you wanted to add it to your toilet library. It is also available as a specially priced (i.e. very cheap) ebook if you are all very modern and own one of those new fangled devices.

If you want to contact Steve, you can drop him a line at 21stcenturydodos@gmail.com.

You can also pay a visit to his blog at http://meandmybigmouth.typepad.com/

21st Century Dodos is also available as an ebook and audiobook.

Still feeling nostalgic? My other book, *Christmas Dodos*, dedicated to treats of Christmases past, is available now as a real book and an ebook.